Bottled Poetry: Verses From The Vine

Vinted and Bottled by
Stephen H. Bass

Spilt Wine Publishing Company
Robinsonville, MS

Bottled Poetry: Verses From The Vine

©2013 Stephen H. Bass
All rights reserved, including the right of reproduction in whole or in part, in any form.

SPILT WINE PUBLISHING COMPANY
Robinsonville, MS
spiltwinebooks.com

No poem was ever written by a drinker of water.
  - Homer (c. 8th century bce)

To Brian
In Memory of
Your Mom
My Mom and Dad
O.L., Bill, and Al

Contents

INTRODUCTION _____ pp 1 - 5

PRAISING AND DEFENDING WINE _____ pp 7 - 20
    Fill the Goblet Again by Lord Byron [8]
    O precious crock . . . by Horace [9]
    "In Praise Of Wine" by Medieval Students [10]
    *When wine I quaff, before my eyes . . .*from *Odes of Anacreon* (Moore) [11]
    A flower-tinted cheek . . . by Hafiz [12]
    The Soul Of Wine by Charles Baudelaire [13]
    Bacchanalian by Victor Daley [14]
    An Exhortation by Li Bai [15]
    To Those Who Serve Us Wine [16]
        On The Death Of The Good Brewer Of Hsuan-Cheng by Li Bai
        And much as Wine has play'd the Infidel . . . by Omar Khayyam
        Feast on wine or fast on water . . . by G.K. Chesterton
    "In Defense Of - The Grape" by Omar Khayyam [17]
    Over the past year I have given up . . . by Cecco Angiolieri [18]
    A Vindication by Li Bai [18]
    Drinking by Abraham Cowley [19]
    A Satisfactory Reform by Ellis Parker Butler [19]

WINE, WOMEN, AND SONG _____ pp 21 – 29
    Who does not love Wine, Women, and Song . . . by Johann Heinrich Voss [22]
    Few things surpass old wine . . . by Lord Byron [22]
    Give me women, wine, and snuff . . . by John Keats [22]
    A Lyric To Myrth by Robert Herrick [22]
    Room 5: The Concert Singer by Robert Service [23]
    Strew me a fragrant bed of leaves . . . from *Odes of Anacreon* (Moore) [24]
    Oh, for a bowl of fat Canary . . . by John Lyly [25]
    Maid of Wu by Li Bai [25]
    Last night, as half asleep I dreaming lay . . . by Hafiz [26]
    Mingle with the genial bowl . . . from *Translations of Anacreon* (Byron) [27]
    "Wine And Love And Lyre " by Medieval Students [28]
    Juan would question further, but she press'd . . . by Lord Byron [29]
    To Bacchus: A Canticle by Robert Herrick [29]

LOVE AND ROMANCE _____ pp. 31 – 44
    A Book of Verses underneath the Bough . . . by Omar Khayyam [32]
    A broken cake, with honey sweet . . . from *Odes of Anacreon* (Moore) [32]
    Song by Paul Laurence Dunbar [32]
    *Go from me. Yet I feel that I shall stand . . .*by Elizabeth Barrett Browning [33]
    To Celia by Ben Jonson [33]

LOVE AND ROMANCE (continued)
The Hypocrite by Witter Bynner [34]
A Grace by Mary Carolyn Davies [34]
If wine and music have the power . . . by Matthew Pryor [35]
Anticipation by Amy Lowell [35]
Mystery by D. H. Lawrence [36]
The Vine by James Thomson [37]
I filled to thee, To thee I drank . . . by Thomas Moore [37]
Veteran And Recruit by Edward Wentwoth Hazewell [38]
The Wine Of Lovers by Charles Baudelaire [39]
A Before and After with W. B. Yeats [39]
   A Drinking Song by William Butler Yeats
   A Deep Sworn Vow by William Butler Yeats
Fill for me a brimming bowl . . . by John Keats [40]
Wisdom by Ernest Dowson [41]
Friend of my soul, this goblet sip . . . by Thomas Moore [41]
"Tis melancholy and a fearful sign . . . by Lord Byron [42]
Bacchanalian by Witter Bynner [42]
The Wine Of The Murderer by Charles Baudelaire [43]

WINE DRINKERS   pp 45 - 55
First: Let's Be Reasonable About This . . . [46]
   Five Reasons For Drinking by Henry Aldrich
   Ad Nepotem by Robert Louis Stevenson
Drinking Alone – Two Perspectives [47]
   A Drinking Song by Henry Carey
   Three With The Moon And His Shadow by Li Bai
Partying With Anacreon [48]
   Give me the harp of epic song . . . from Odes of Anacreon (Moore)
   I pray thee by the gods above . . . from Odes of Anacreon (Moore)
   To-day I'll haste to quaff my wine . . . from Odes of Anacreon (Moore)
Partying With Li Bai [49]
   A Mountain Revelry by Li Bai
   With A Man Of Leisure by Li Bai
   A Midnight Farewell by Li Bai
   The Solitude Of Night by Li Bai
The Morning After [50]
   Man being reasonable, must get drunk . . . by Lord Byron
   Bacchus, let me drink no more . . . by Robert Herrick
Wine And Friendship
   Lawrence of virtuous father, virtuous son by John Milton [51]
   On The Yo-Yang Tower With His Friend, Chia by Li Bai [51]
   To James Corry, Esq.: On His Making Me A Present Of A Wine Strainer by
      Thomas Moore [52]
   Parting At A Tavern Of Chin-Ling by Li Bai [52]

WINE DRINKERS (continued)
  WINE SNOBBERY
    Lé Dîner by A. H. Clough [53]
    Fish by Amy Lowell [54]
    The Gourd by Paul Laurence Dunbar [54]

WINE MUSINGS _____ pp. 57 - 73
  For Is and Is-not though with rule and line... by Omar Khayyam [58]
  Lines Inscribed Upon A Cup Formed From A Skull by Lord Byron [58]
  You know, my Friends, with what a brave Carouse... by Omar Khayyam [59]
  The Mote by Bliss Carman and Richard Hovey [59]
  Fill A Glass With Golden Wine by William Ernest Henley [60]
  Day and Night by Victor Daley [60]
  The Inn Of Earth by Sara Teasdale [61]
  A Blockhead by Amy Lowell [61]
  Fair Hope! our earlier heaven... by Abraham Cowley [62]
  Good Hope by Ralph Waldo Emerson [62]
  Happiness by Amy Lowell [63]
  Hymn To Beauty by Charles Baudelaire [64]
  Cana by James Freeman Clarke [65]
  To Our Lord Upon The Water Made Wine by Richard Crashaw [65]
  Past And Future by Elizabeth Barrett Browning [66]
  Waste not your Hour, nor in the vain pursuit... by Omar Khayyam [67]
  The Mystic by Witter Bynner [67]
  And this I know: whether the one True Light... by Omar Khayyam [67]
  Come, Send Round The Wine by Thomas Moore [68]
  Ne'er talk of Wisdom's gloomy schools... by Thomas Moore [68]
  Be Drunk (a prose poem) by Charles Baudelaire [69]
  Bacchus by Ralph Waldo Emerson [70]
  Ode To A Nightingale by John Keats [72]

POETRY AND POETS _____ pp. 75 - 87
  "*Wine And The Art Of Poetry I*" by Medieval Students [76]
  Omarism by Victor Daley [76]
  "*Wine And The Art Of Poetry II*" by Medieval Students [77]
  The Wine by Sara Teasdale [78]
  Vintage by Mary Carolyn Davies [78]
  Think not that Wine against good verse offends... by John Milton [79]
  The Wine Of The Solitary by Charles Baudelaire [80]
  Whitman And Emerson by Marguerite Wilkinson [81]
  To Meng Haojan by Li Bai [82]
  To Li Bai On A Spring Day by Du Fu [82]
  Omar Khayyam by Richard Le Gallienne [83]
  The Thyrsus: To Franz Liszt (a prose poem) by Charles Baudelaire [84]
  Eight Immortals of the Wine Cup by Du Fu [85]
  His Farewell To Sack by Robert Herrick [86]

BAD TIMES _____ pp. 89 – 98
    God made man... by Anonymous [90]
    Solitude by Ella Wheeler Wilcox [90]
    Disappointment by Thomas Stephen Collier [91]
    Three Clusters Of Grapes by Giovanni Pascoli [91]
    Dregs by Ernest Dowson [91]
    Take hence the bowl... by Thomas Moore [92]
    Chinese Poet Among Barbarians by John Gould Fletcher [92]
    To Em-mei's "The Unmoving Cloud" by Tao Yuanming [93)
    The Wine Of The Rag-Pickers by Charles Baudelaire [94]
    The Deluge by G. K. Chesterton [95]
    Arise, oh Cupbearer, rise! and bring... by Hafiz [96]
    Alchemy by Sara Teasdale [97]
    Within this goblet, rich and deep ... from *Odes of Anacreon* (Moore) [97]
    Awakening From Sleep by Li Bai [98]

AGING _____ pp. 99 – 105
    Mix me, child, a cup divine... from *Odes of Anacreon* (Moore) [100]
    Spring And Autumn by Thomas Moore [100]
    Away, away ye men of rules... from *Odes of Anacreon* (Moore) [101]
    Born I was to meet with age... by Robert Herrick [101]
    Resignation by Bliss Carman and Richard Hovey [102]
    Epicurean by William James Linton [102]
    The Lyre Of Anacreon by Oliver Wendell Holmes [103]
    When I behold the festive train... from *Odes of Anacreon* (Moore) [104]
    Before The Cask Of Wine by Li Bai [105]
    Tis true, my fading years decline... from *Odes of Anacreon* (Moore) [105]

FINAL TOASTS _____ pp. 107 – 114
    Champagne, 1914-15 by Alan Seeger [108]
    The Voiceless by Oliver Wendall Holmes [110]
    The Legacy by Thomas Moore [111]
    They are not long, the weeping and the laughter... by Ernest Dowson [112]
    The Great Misgiving by William Watson [112]
    From the garden of Heaven a western breeze... by Hafiz [113]
    "Sans Wine – Sans Song – Sans Singer" by Omar Khayyam [114]
    "A Final Toast" by Omar Khayyam [114]

NEW PRESSINGS by S.H. Bass _____ pp. 115– 132
    What Can Be Said About Both Wine And Poetry [116]
    Inspiration [116]
    Wine, Thy Name Is Woman [117]
    An Altar Boy's Lament [118]
    My New Trinity [118]
    Wine Knows No Winter [119]
    Ode To White Zinfandel [120]

NEW PRESSINGS (continued)
   From The Cellar [121]
   A Wine Poem [122]
   Wine-In-A-Bag-In-A-Box [123]
   Three Demis [124]
   Bacchanalia [125]
   A Sonnet Sequence [126]
      Sonnet #1
      Sonnet #1,234
   Steve's Guide To Love And Romance
      Step 1: Meet Her: *The Discovery* [127]
      Step 2: Talk To Her: *Somewhere In The Wine* [128]
      Step 3: Regret Talking To Her: *Buy With Bread . . . Sell With Cheese* [129]
      Step 4: Fell Sorry For Yourself: *Spilt Wine* [130]
      Step 5: Write Some Poetry: *The Poet's Wine* (a prose poem) [132]

Envoy by Robert Louis Stevenson [133]

Index by Poets and Translators [135]

Acknowledgements, Resources, and The Public Domain [139]

vintagewinepoems.com [143]

A Final Word [145]

Special Acknowledgements [147]

INTRODUCTION

Perhaps it started when one of our earliest ancestors emerged from some forgotten cave grunting praises for the juice of found grapes gone bad. Ever since, we *homo sapiens* have been praising, condemning, defending, and metaphorically using and abusing wine in our poetry. The wine poem has been around since the inception of verse, leaving us with a collection of poetry that represents a virtual history of the poetic arts: from the lyrics of ancient Greece, accompanied by the ancient lyre, to the birth of free verse, the "prose poem" – and beyond.

Bottled Poetry: Verses From The Vine is more than a poetic celebration of wine, revelry, and romance, as one might think when contemplating the concept "wine poem". Amid the celebration and revelry, you will find poems that use wine as metaphors, fingers pointing to sometimes poignant, sometimes frivolous moons. Partying and parting . . . good times and bad times . . . love, war, non-violence, and murder . . . friends, lovers, and family . . . the silly and the profound . . . the sacred and the profane . . . all somehow linked to a goblet, a bottle, a vineyard – to wine.

Does the mere mention of wine a wine poem make? For the purposes of this project[*], not all "wine poems" serve-up wine as the main topic or the major metaphor. Wine may serve as a single, yet vital, brush-stroke within a larger picture poetically painted. Like on our tables, wine's role may be as an accompaniment to a larger feast that a poet presents.

Admittedly, this is a broad definition of the term "wine poem", but it is one that makes this book more than a poetic conversation about "wine, revelry, and romance", more than a compendium of drinking songs. The wine poems presented here are as varied as to type, style, depth, and, yes, quality, as the wine selection in your favorite wine shop. Practically every form and style of poetry is represented here, from epigrams to epics – from appellations that collectively cover our globe.

You will find within these pages wine poems that rate among the finest examples of the poetic art. These poems we haughtily classify as "Literature": those "fine wines" one must sip and savor, swashing the words around in one's mind (and mouth) a bit, in order to enjoy the depth and subtle flavors that the poet wishes to impart. These poems will give you pause, leave you with the suspicion that there is more here than a quick gulp reveals. With fine poetry, like fine wine, the imbiber must take his time. Patience is a virtue. Some poems call for quiet meditation: open them slowly and let them breathe.

---

[*]   *Bottled Poetry: Verses From The Vine* is part of a larger project that includes the website vintagewinepoems.com, the Vintage Wine Poems Channel on Vimeo, and the publications of Spilt Wine Publishing Company (spiltwinebooks.com).

Other wine poems are simple, clever turns of phrase – set to rhythm and rhyme. These, which are not "easy" to write, are like the quaffing wines of Beaujolais: they tend to be light and a bit "fruity" ("flowery" is another "tasting note" that comes to mind). Their aim is a quick smile, a moment's repast in our day. This sometimes, perhaps most times, is enough.

The Art of Translation

Poetry is an art form where the sound and rhythm of words are as important as their meaning. Whether the poem be spoken aloud or in the reader's head, it is the very sound and rhythm of the words that impart that meaning. Linguistic differences between languages (the stresses, the pitch, the accentuation, etc. of the spoken word) coupled with metaphors whose meaning are found in the traditions of a foreign culture, make the translation of poetry a monumental task. Whether the original poet wrote in ancient Greek or modern French, the translation of poetry is as much art as the poetry writing itself. The argument is made, that to truly benefit from the full measure of a poet's work, it must be read in it's original language.

With the poetry of the ancient cultures, the challenges facing the translator increase. Often the translator is faced with fragments of poems, third party quotations, and ambiguous authorship issues. "Filling in the blanks" with lines and stanzas of the translator's own invention is not uncommon or unwarranted. The translator's goal is to stay true to the original author's voice and intent, while producing a readable piece of poesy that is not swallowed by footnotes and parenthetical clarifications. As with all antiques, authenticity becomes an issue, but with poetry translations from ancient cultures, the best we can hope for are quality replicas, painted plaster casts of original (often broken) artifacts of gold.

With all this in mind, it should not surprise you that there is often controversy surrounding translations. Most of these controversies involve the retention of the original poet's intent and meaning, a slippery slope with a medium such as poetry when meaning and intent can purposely be multilayered and elusive. There are those among the literati whose solution to this conundrum (noting that, especially with poetry, something is always "lost in translation") is to place translation as a separate art form, the translator being a creative force that should feel quite free to express himself in his art.

My personal opinion, as a consumer, is that as long as credit due is given to the artists involved, I'll leave the " 'tis and 'tis not's" to others for discussion over their jug of wine. I will like or dislike the poetry before me over mine. As you encounter translations in the pages ahead (approximately 1/3 of the poems), keep in mind the unique and creative role of the translator of poetry. There are alternative translations for every non-English poet that appears here. Any of the more interesting issues involving these translations will be dealt with in the "Back Label" comments that are scattered throughout this volume.

BACK LABEL

You read them at the wine shop. They tend to give historical data, tasting notes, trivia, and propaganda about the wine that's in the bottle and the wine-maker and the wine-making process that put it there. This is also the function of these "back labels" in *Bottled Poetry*, focusing on rhymes, rhyme-makers, and the rhyme-making process that put them here. I will try to keep the propaganda to a minimum

---

vintagewinepoems.com

FitzGerald's Omar Khayyam

A prime example of the controversies surrounding translations can be found with the poetry of Omar Khayyam and the famous translation of his works by Edward FitzGerald. Persian poet, mathematician, and astronomer Omar Khayyam is believed to have written about a thousand poetic couplets and quatrains (rubai's). The verse you encounter in *Bottled Poetry: Verses from the Vine* (9 wine poems consisting of a total 19 quatrains) are from *The Rubáiyát of Omar Khayyam translated into English verse by Edward FitzGerald*, a book first published in 1859. This became an immensely popular book, to the point of attracting parodies well into the next century.

By FitzGerald's own acknowledgment, this work is often a paraphrase of the original. For instance, a direct translation a Khayyam fragment reads:

> Forsake not the book, the lover's lips and the green bank of the field,
> Ere that the earth enfold thee in its bosom.

With FitzGerald's translation, we get one of his and Omar's most well-known verses:

> A Book of Verses underneath the Bough,
> A Jug of Wine, a Loaf of Bread – and Thou
>   Beside me singing in the Wilderness –
> Oh, Wilderness were Paradise enow!

While in such instances, the more accurate description for such poetry might be "inspired by" rather than "a translation of", most critics agree that FitzGerald captured the spirit of Khayyam's work. These Khayyam/FitzGerald quatrains form an important part of the history of poetry and poetry publishing.

There Be Gods Here!

Greek mythology, and its copycat Roman mythology, have long been rich vineyards to which writers have gone to pluck a storyline, a character, and a metaphor. The wine poet who wishes to walk among these gods has two deities directly responsible for his areas of interest. Dionysus (Bacchus in Rome) is the god of wine. Apollo (same name in both Greek and Roman mythology) is the god of poetry, among many other areas of dominion.

Dionysus first gifted the earth with grape vines and was a favorite among the ancients. Who wouldn't love a god whose central act of worship was a wine party? The most important members of his entourage were the Maenads (also called bacchantes), beautiful and seductive women who could turn to extreme acts of violence under the spell of Dionysus (and his wine).

Apollo's domain included prophesy, the sun, and music (poetry). The Muses were nine daughters of Zeus (Jupiter in Rome, the head god) who inspired poetry and the arts, and hung out with Apollo. Apollo and the Muses are often pictured together. Apollo is often depicted holding a lyre, the symbol for the lyric poetry that dominated ancient Greece and Rome.

There are over 20 major gods ruling the Greek and Roman universe, with a vast assortment of Graces, Satyrs, nymphs, and other un-earthy beings joining in the dance. Throw in the myths of other cultures and the quaint, "literary", sometimes archaic, terms poets draw upon to meet meter and rhyme demands and a mini-dictionary could accompany this anthology. Look to the "Back Label" sidebar for guidance.

Poets have no loyalty to a specific religion, so you will see them (and their translators) mix Greek and Roman names together in the service of meter, alliteration, assonance, and rhyme. Thus, for instance, you will have a Greek voice call upon Bacchus, the Roman god of wine, because "Dionysus" has too many syllables. The only name you have to carry away from this introduction is Dionysus/Bacchus, whose name appears as often as "bowl", "grape", and "vine" in the pages that follow.

Themes

I have divided *Bottled Poetry* into nine (9) themed categories, because that's what they tell me anthology editors do. Of course, the poets did not write to fit neatly into my themes, so there is some over-lap. There is an introduction to each themed section, because, once again, that is what anthology editors do. This is where you will find most of my pontifications ("Back Labels" are good for this, too). Read them. I am a pretty good pontificator.

Seriously, though, the order in which these wine poems are presented is not by accident. Many hours of thought were spent blending and pairing the wide variety of poetry you will find here to achieve the most enjoyable read. So, I want you to start with the first poem and read them in order. To do otherwise would be an insult to me and the entire anthology editing community.

OK . . .so you are not going to do that. Skip around. Themes were actually designed to help you do just that! I was only kidding in the above paragraph (any sentence I begin with the word "seriously" usually is not). Poems that complement one another, at times by contrasting one another, are in close proximity to one another, within themes, where they hover.

The first nine sections of *Bottled Poetry* are devoted to vintage wine poems, that poetry and those poets who have stood the test of time (although some poems do carry a little "sediment" from bygone days that the "Back Label" will aid in filtering). The final section, *New Pressings*, is the poetry of S.H. Bass . . . me. These are the poems that actually got this project started. Feel free to skip there right now.

Editorial Peccadilloes

Poets do not always title their poems. Sometimes they are part of a collection and are just simply numbered , as in "Sonnet #1,234". In *Bottled Poetry*, a wine poem may be an excerpt from a larger work that may or may not have been titled. For clarity, with these untitled poems I have used the first line of the poem (or a fragment thereof) as it's title. When listed in a table of contents or index, *"Tis melancholy, and a fearful sign"* is a more informative designation for the verse by Lord Byron than **"from *Don Juan*: canto II, stanza 5"** The same holds true for "Sonnet #1,234". Origins of these wine poems are duly noted.

On a few occasions I have taken the liberty of titling a wine poem with my own words. You can spot these by my use of "quotation marks". These are invariably multi-stanza poems lifted from a larger work, where the opening line does not describe the essence of the wine poem.

You have probably already noticed that I use the pronoun "I" instead of the editorial "we". I also use the masculine "he", "his", and "him" when a sentence is not gender specific. I find the use of the editorial "we" annoying and misleading. It is just me. I find the use of he/she (or she/he) to be cumbersome. When I read them or write them in such a manner, it makes me want to — what the third person singular pronouns (she/he/it) sound like when you say them together real fast. I am not an egotist or a chauvinist, or should I have said "we"?

". . .and the wine is bottled poetry."

For those of you who have wandered the vine lands of the Napa Valley in California, the most well known reference to wine and poetry can be found on billboards, welcome signs, and tourist brochures of the area: *". . . and the wine is bottled poetry."* The quote is from the novelist, poet, and essayist Robert Louis Stevenson (1850 -1894). Best known for his novel *Treasure Island* and his classic tale of *The Strange Case of Dr. Jekyll and Mr. Hyde*, Stevenson was also a wine enthusiast.

In *The Silverado Squatters* (1883), he takes the reader on a tour of what will become the wine country of California. The Gold Rush is over. The phylloxera pestilence is ravaging the vineyards of Europe. His prose is both poetic and prophetic. It is from his observations that the title for this anthology is drawn:

> *Wine in California is still in the experimental stage . . . the beginning of vine-planting is like the beginning of mining for the precious metals: the wine-grower also "Prospects". One corner of land after another is tried with one kind of grape after another. This is a failure; that is better; a third best. So, bit by bit, they grope about for their Clos Vougeot and Lafite. Those lodes and pockets of earth, more precious than the precious ores, that yield inimitable fragrance and soft fire; those virtuous Bonanzas, where the soil has sublimated under sun and stars to something finer, and the wine is bottled poetry: these still lie undiscovered; chaparral conceals, thicket embowers them; the miner chips the rock and wanders farther, and the grizzly muses undisturbed. But there they bide their hour, awaiting their Columbus; and nature nurses and prepares them. The smack of Californian earth shall linger on the palate of your grandson.*

I am no Columbus, but I hope you enjoy my discoveries.

Stephen H. Bass
Strayhorn, Mississippi
Fall, 2013

Praising and Defending Wine

Wine is *amorous, gregarious, auspicious, delicious, propitious, faithful, blessed . . . a truth serum, memory cleanser, mind focus-er, love potion . . . a curer of headache, heartache, backache . . . bearer of truth, wit, courage, hope, love* . . .and therefore, oh so taxable.

To praise wine is to defend wine, and in defending it we must often turn to praise. The tendency to hyperbole duly noted, the following poems extol the virtues of wine, often under the sights of teetotalers, who seem to make their first appearance alongside Dionysus as he gifted the world with grape vines. In fact, the resurgence of the wine poem in the 19th century can be credited to the growth of temperance movements in America and Europe. For this, I guess, we owe these grape-haters a nod of thanks.

Some of the poetry that follows is written in praise of drunkenness. Once again noting the poet's tendency toward hyperbole, let's face it: wine intoxicates. It contains a mind altering, mood altering, motor skills altering drug: alcohol. I have been drunk with wine. I will be drunk with wine again. This will not happen tonight. It may not happen for months, even years (doubtful) . . .but on some occasion, either by being "caught in the moment" or by design, I will get drunk. Not falling-down, passing out drunk. But more of what I like to call the "poet laureate of the bar" drunk, charmingly uninhibited and an embarrassment to my sober self.

During these periods, I will not operate a motor vehicle. I will flirt with women I shouldn't, perhaps your wife. (I will not get into fisticuffs for this privilege, however.) I will say, quite loudly, both stupid and insightful things, and will defend both with equal vigor. My friends will try to quiet me. My good friends will egg me on. I will not be so drunk that I cannot feign sobriety, but I will avoid sharing this skill with an officer of the law. I will not operate a motor vehicle.

Do I, on these occasions, drink to excess? Can one cheer too loudly for the home team? Can one be caught up in the rapture of a sonnet, a sonata, or a sunrise to excess? I am not talking here of a loss of control, but a loss of this daily shell in which we grind out our daily lives. When our daily lives are under the control of the bottle, or the idolized sports team, poet, musician, or "star" . . . this is when we have a problem. With the former, the disease is called alcoholism. With the latter intoxicants, the disease is called fanaticism. I now direct you to the "Wine Musings" section of this anthology and Charles Baudelaire's prose poem *Be Drunk* (p. 69) for further discussion.

Fill The Goblet Again

Fill the goblet again! for I never before
Felt the glow which now gladdens my heart to its core;
Let us drink! – who would not? – since, through life's varied round,
In the goblet alone no deception is found.

I have tried in its turn all that life can supply;
I have basked in the beam of a dark rolling eye;
I have loved! – who has not? – but what heart can declare
That Pleasure existed while Passion was there?

In the days of my youth, when the heart's in its spring,
And dreams that Affection can never take wing,
I had friends! – who has not? – but what tongue will avow,
That friends, rosy wine! are so faithful as thou?

The heart of a mistress some boy may estrange,
Friendship shifts with the sunbeam – thou never canst change;
Thou grows old – who does not? – but on earth what appears,
Whose virtues, like thine, still increase with its years?

Yet if blest to the utmost that Love can bestow,
Should a rival bow down to our idol below,
We are jealous! – who's not? – thou hast no such alloy;
For the more that enjoy thee, the more we enjoy.

Then the season of youth and its vanities past,
For refuge we fly to the goblet at last;
There we find – do we not? – in the flow of the soul,
That truth, as of yore, is confined to the bowl.

When the box of Pandora was opened on earth,
And Misery's triumph commenced over Mirth,
Hope was left, – was she not? – but the goblet we kiss,
And care not for Hope, who are certain of bliss.

Long life to the grape! for when summer is flown,
The age of our nectar shall gladden our own:
We must die – who shall not? – May our sins be forgiven,
And Hebe shall never be idle in Heaven.

Lord Byron (1788—1824)

BACK LABEL

Some poems scream to be read aloud. Imagine Lord Byron (a partier of renown), giving an "over-the-top" recitation of this poem amidst the Lords and Ladies of his day. I dare you to do the same at your next wine gathering!

[stanza 7]: According to Greek mythology, Pandora, the first women in a perfect world, was given a box by Zeus and instructed not to open it. Humans being human, Pandora opened the box, which contained all the maladies of our present world – plus the one relief from them all: hope. (As Byron points out, "hope" is unnecessary in a perfect world, where we are "certain of bliss").

Hebe (last line) was cup-bearer of Mount Olympus – sommelier to the gods!

O precious crock, whose summers date,
Like mine, from Manlius' consulate,
I know not whether in your breast
Lie maudlin wail or merry jest,
Or sudden choler, or the fire
Of tipsy Love's insane desire,
Or fumes of soft caressing sleep,
Or what more potent charms you keep,
But this I know, your ripened power
Befits some choicely festive hour!
A cup peculiarly mellow
Corvinus asks; so come, old fellow,
From your time-honored bin descend,
And let me gratify my friend!
No churl is he, your charms to slight,
Though most intensely erudite:
And even old Cato's worth, we know,
Took from good wine a nobler glow.

Your magic power of wit can spread
The halo round a dullard's head,
Can make the sage forget his care,
His bosom's inmost thoughts unbare,
And drown his solemn-faced pretense
Beneath your blithesome influence.
Bright hope you bring and vigor back
To minds outworn upon the rack,
And put such courage in the brain,
As makes the poor be men again,
Whom neither tyrants' wrath affrights,
Nor all their bristling satellites.

Bacchus, and Venus, so that she
Bring only frank festivity,
With sister Graces in her train,
Twining close in lovely chain,
And gladsome tapers' living light,
Shall spread your treasures over the night,
Till Phoebus the red East unbars,
And puts to rout the trembling stars.

> *Ode 3*
> Horace (65 - 8bce)
> translation by Theodore Martin (1816-1909)

BACK LABEL

Horace is addressing a "crock" of wine that shares his birthday, the year of "Manlius' consulate" (65bce)

Poets can be a wordy lot. The abridged version of this poem: WINE IS GREAT! (stanzas 1 and 2) LET'S PARTY 'TILL THE SUN COMES UP! (last stanza)

[first stanza] Cato: Roman official and noted historian, known as "Cato, the Elder".

[last stanza] Venus: the goddess of love. The Graces: three sister goddesses who could grant beauty, charm, and happiness. Phoebus: another name for Apollo, here in his role as the sun god: you know, the dude in charge of pulling the sun across the sky with his chariot.

"In Praise of Wine"

Wine the good and bland, thou blessing
Of the good, the bad's distressing,
Sweet of taste by all confessing,
Hail, thou world's felicity!
Hail thy hue, life's gloom dispelling;
Hail thy taste, all tastes excelling;
By thy power, in this thy dwelling
Deign to make us drunk with thee!

Oh, how blest for bounteous uses
Is the birth of pure vine-juices!
Safe's the table which produces
Wine in goodly quality.
Oh, in color how auspicious!
Oh, in odor how delicious!
In the mouth how sweet, propitious
To the tongue enthralled by thee!

Blest the man who first thee planted,
Called thee by thy name enchanted!
He whose cups have never been scanted
Dreads no danger that may be.
Blest the belly where thou bidest!
Blest the tongue where thou residest!
Blest the mouth through which thou glidest,
And the lips thrice blest by thee!

    Medieval Students (c. 12th century)
    translation by John Addington Symonds (1840 – 1893)

BACK LABEL

Who were these Wandering Students? They were men, and for the most part young men, traveling from university to university in search of knowledge. Far from their homes, without responsibilities, light of purse and light of heart, careless and pleasure-seeking, they ran a free, disreputable course, frequenting taverns at least as much as lecture rooms, more capable of pronouncing judgment upon wine or women than upon a problem of divinity or logic.
    - John Addington Symonds

College life hasn't changed much over the centuries

When wine I quaff, before my eyes
Dreams of poetic glory rise;
And freshened by the goblet's dews,
My soul invokes the heavenly Muse.
When wine I drink, all sorrow's o'er;
I think of doubts and fears no more;
But scatter to the railing wind
Each gloomy phantom of the mind.

When I drink wine, the ethereal boy,
Bacchus himself, partakes my joy;
And while we dance through vernal bowers,
Whose every breath comes fresh from flowers,
In wine he makes my senses swim,
Till the gale breathes of naught but him!

Again I drink, – and, lo, there seems
A calmer light to fill my dreams;
The lately ruffled wreath I spread
With steadier hand around my head;
Then take the lyre, and sing "how blest
The life of him who lives at rest!"

But then comes witching wine again,
With glorious woman in its train;
And, while rich perfumes round me rise,
That seem the breath of woman's sighs,
Bright shapes of every hue and form
Upon my kindling fancy swarm,
Till the whole world of beauty seems
To crowd into my dazzled dreams!

When thus I drink, my heart refines,
And rises as the cup declines;
Rises in the genial flow,
That none but social spirits know,
When, with young revelers, round the bowl,
The old themselves grow young in soul!

Oh, when I drink, true joy is mine,
There's bliss in every drop of wine.
All other blessings I have known,
I scarcely dared to call my own;
But this the Fates can never destroy,
Till death overshadows all my joy.

    Ode 50 from *Odes of Anacreon* (1800)
    translation by Thomas Moore (1779-1852)

BACK LABEL

Anacreon of Teos (c. 570-485bce) was a Greek poet known in his day as the master of the wine poem (as well as poems about love, feasting, and roses). We know of him today through the few fragments of his poetry that have survived and via other writers of antiquity who speak of him. Over the centuries, however, his name has been attached to a volume of poetry that spans some 600 years, including works that modern linguistic detectives identify as other than Greek in origin. This mass of poetry cannot all be accurately credited to the bard of Teos who died in 485 bce.

"Anacreon", through either innocent error or marketing mischief ("Anacreon" was a strong brand name) has become the pseudonym of these unidentifiable poets of antiquity. These poems speak in a common lyrical style of wine, revelry, and romance as one imagines them celebrated in ancient Greece or Rome. They form the archetype of what most folks envision when contemplating the concept "wine poem".

The majority of the poems traditionally credited to "Anacreon" in this volume (see page 27 for an Anacreon translation by Lord Byron), come from Thomas Moore. Moore first received notice as a writer for his translation, *Odes of Anacreon* (1800). Most scholars whimsically refer to these poems of the Moore translation as "Anacreon of Moore" (as opposed to "Anacreon of Teos"). Upon reading Moore's commentary in his *Odes of Anacreon*, it is obvious that Moore was aware of these authorship issues.

A flower-tinted cheek, the flowery close
Of the fair earth, these are enough for me
Enough that in the meadow wanes and grows
The shadow of a graceful cypress-tree.
I am no lover of hypocrisy;
Of all the treasures that the earth can boast,
A brimming cup of wine I prize the most
                  This is enough for me!

To them that here renowned for virtue live,
A heavenly palace is the meet reward;
To me, the drunkard and the beggar, give
The temple of the grape with red wine stored!
Beside a river seat thee on the sward;
It floweth past so flows thy life away,
So sweetly, swiftly, fleets our little day
                  Swift, but enough for me!

Look upon all the gold in the world's mart,
On all the tears the world hath shed in vain;
Shall they not satisfy thy craving heart?
I have enough of loss, enough of gain;
I have my Love, what more can I obtain?
Mine is the joy of her companionship
Whose healing lip is laid upon my lip
                  This is enough for me!

I pray thee send not forth my naked soul
From its poor house to seek for Paradise
Though heaven and earth before me God unroll,
Back to thy village still my spirit flies.
And, Hafiz, at the door of Kismet lies
No just complaint a mind like water clear,
A song that swells and dies upon the ear,
                    These are enough for thee!

#6 from *Poems From The Divan of Hafiz* (1897)
Hafiz (c. 1320-1389)
translation by Gertrude Bell (1868-1926)

BACK LABEL

Hafiz and Omar Khayyam are two Persian poets who appear here as wine poets. (Persia consisted of lands that basically covers modern day Iran). Notable objections might come from the Muslim world, where the orthodoxy take issue with any support of alcohol. Critics point to a long history of religious writings that metaphorically link wine with mystical union with God, and intoxication with spiritual awakening and fervor (including a rich Sufi tradition within Islam). However, both Hafiz and Khayyam undeniably speak of the joy of the everyday use of wine and denounce those who would seek to deny such pleasures. I would align these religious critics with those fundamentalists from my own Christian tradition who would claim that Jesus' wine miracle at Cana or the goblet he held at the Last Supper involved some substance other than an alcoholic beverage. These folks would have us reverse Jesus' miracle at Cana, and turn wine into water.

Regardless of your interpretation, a poem that employs wine as a metaphor, whether that finger points to heaven, hell, or mere earthly delights – by my definition – is a wine poem.

[last stanza]: Kismit, in Islam, refers to the will of Allah.

The Soul Of Wine

One eve in the bottle sang the soul of wine:
"Man, unto thee, dear disinherited,
I sing a song of love and light divine
Prisoned in glass beneath my seals of red.

"I know thou laborest on the hill of fire,
In sweat and pain beneath a flaming sun,
To give the life and soul my vines desire,
And I am grateful for thy labors done.

"For I find joys unnumbered when I lave
The throat of man by travail long outworn,
And his hot bosom is a sweeter grave
Of sounder sleep than my cold caves forlorn.

"Hearest thou not the echoing Sabbath sound?
The hope that whispers in my trembling breast?
Thy elbows on the table! gaze around;
Glorify me with joy and be at rest.

"To thy wife's eyes I'll bring their long-lost gleam,
I'll bring back to thy child his strength and light,
To him, life's fragile athlete, I will seem
Rare oil that firms his muscles for the fight.

"I flow in man's heart as ambrosia flows;
The grain the eternal Sower casts in the sod.
From our first loves the first fair verse arose,
Flower-like aspiring to the heavens and God!"

    Charles Baudelaire (1821–1867)
    translation by F. P. Sturm (1879-1943)

Bacchanalian

I pity him who has not swung
The Thyrsus in the air,
And followed Bacchus, blithe and young,
With vine-leaves in his hair;
And heard the Maenads sing.
And the mad cymbals ring.

I pity those who have to walk
In sober ways and sad,
And keep a guard upon their talk
Lest men should think them mad.
Or careless speech should show
The felon thought below.

When in my goblet, blithe and gay,
The bearded bubbles wink,
For all poor souls like this I pray
That they may learn to drink,
And like a rose in rain
Open shut heart and brain.

Who does not drink he does not know,
And he will never find,
What merry fellows live below
The surface of his mind:
These other men to me
Are right good company.
If beings of Mythology
Could live at my commands
Briareus I'd choose to be,
Who had a hundred hands:
And every hand of mine
Would hold a pint of wine.

And of those beakers ninety-nine
With white wine and with red
Should brim for dear old friends of mine.
The living and the dead.
By Pluto there would be
A noble revelry!

Then let us unto Bacchus sing
Evoe! up and down –
For Bacchus is the wisest king
Who ever wore a crown:
His vine leaves hide from view
More wit than Plato knew.

    Victor Daley (1858-1905)

> **BACK LABEL**
>
> The mythical and earthly followers of Bacchus were known as Bacchanalians.
>
> A thyrsus is a vine-covered staff carried by the followers of Bacchus.
>
> Another wine poem bearing the same name comes to us from Witter Bynner. In his Bacchanalian, Bynner focuses on a specific segment of the followers of Bacchus, the female devotees known as Maenads or Bacchantes (see page 42).

An Exhortation

Do you not see the waters of the Yellow River
Come flowing from the sky?
The swift stream pours into the sea and returns never-more.
Do you not see high on yonder tower
A white-haired one sorrowing before his bright mirror?
In the morning those locks were like black silk,
In the evening they are all snow.
Let us, while we may, taste the old delights,
And leave not the gold cask of wine
To stand alone in the moonlight!

Gods have bestowed our genius on us;
They will also find its use some day.
Be not loath, therefore, to spend
Even a thousand gold pieces! Your money will come back.
Kill the sheep, slay the ox, and carouse!
Truly you should drink three hundred cups in a round!

Come, Chin, my friend!
Dear Tan-chiu, too.
To you I offer wine, you must not refuse it.
Now I will sing a snatch of song. Lend ear and hearken!
Little I prize gongs and drums and sweet-meats,
I desire only the long ecstasy of wine,
And desire not to awaken.

Since the days of old, the wise and the good
Have been left alone in their solitude,
While merry drinkers have achieved enviable fame.
The king of Chen would feast in ancient days
At his Palace of Peace and Pleasure;
Ten thousand measures of wine there were,
And reckless revelry forever.

Now let you and me buy wine to-day!
Why say we have not the price?
My horse spotted with five flowers,
My fur-coat worth a thousand pieces of gold,
These I will take out, and call my boy
To barter them for sweet wine.
And with you twain, let me forget
The sorrow of ten thousand ages!

   Li Bai (701 - 762)
   translation by Shigeyoshi Obata (1888-1971)

BACK LABEL

The wine of ancient China was usually made from fermented grains, but wines from grapes, plums, pears, and other fruits were also available. And while wine was served in small wine-cups about the size of a shot glass, and tradition held that the wine be taken in one gulp, such numbers as "300 cups in a round" (2nd stanza) must be taken as poetic hyperbole.

TO THOSE WHO SERVE US WINE

From Three Different Eras . . . From Three Different Continents . . .

On The Death Of The Good Brewer Of Hsuan-Cheng

So, old man, you're down where the yellow waters flow.
Well, I imagine you are still brewing the "Old Springtime."
But since there's no Li Bai on the Terrace of Night,
To what sort of people do you sell your wine?

> Li Bai (701 - 762)
> translation by Shigeyoshi Obata (1888-1971)

> **BACK LABEL**
>
> The Chinese often gave brand names to their wine that invoked the season of Spring.
>
> Both "where the yellow waters flow" and "Terrace of the Night" are traditional references to the abode of our deceased ancestors.

And much as Wine has play'd the Infidel,
And robbed me of my Robe of Honor – Well,
   I wonder often what the Vintners buy
One half so precious as the stuff they sell.

> Quatrain 95 from *The Rubáiyát of Omar Khayyam -5th Edition* (1889)
> Omar Khayyam (1048 - 1131)
> translation by Edward FitzGerald (1809–1883)

Feast on wine or fast on water
And your honor shall stand sure,
God Almighty's son and daughter
He the valiant, she the pure;
If an angel out of heaven
Brings you other things to drink,
Thank him for his kind attentions,
Go and pour them down the sink.

> from *The Song of Right and Wrong* (lns 1-8)
> G.K. Chesterton (1874 - 1936)

> **BACK LABEL**
>
> The complete poem, *The Song of Right and Wrong* by G.K. Chesterton can be found at vintagewinepoems.com.

"In Defense Of – The Grape!"

And lately, by the Tavern Door agape,
Came shining through the Dusk an Angel Shape
    Bearing a Vessel on his Shoulder; and
He bid me taste of it; and 'twas – the Grape!

The Grape that can with Logic absolute
The Two-and-Seventy jarring Sects confute:
    The sovereign Alchemist that in a trice
Life's leaden metal into Gold transmute;

Why, be this Juice the growth of God, who dare
Blaspheme the twisted tendril as a Snare?
    A Blessing, we should use it, should we not?
And if a Curse – why, then, Who set it there?

I must abjure the Balm of Life, I must,
Scared by some After-reckoning ta'en on trust,
    Or lured with Hope of some Diviner Drink,
To fill the Cup – when crumbled into Dust!

Of threats of Hell and Hopes of Paradise!
One thing at least is certain – This Life flies;
    One thing is certain and the rest is Lies;
The Flower that once has blown for ever dies.

Strange, is it not? that of the myriads who
Before us pass'd the door of Darkness through,
    Not one returns to tell us of the Road,
Which to discover we must travel too.

    Quatrains 58,59, 61–64 from *The Rubáiyát of Omar Khayyam -5th Edition* (1889)
    Omar Khayyam (1048 -1131)
    translation by Edward FitzGerald (1809–1883)

Back Label

[stanza 2]: "The Two-and-Seventy jarring Sects" is a reference to the 72 religions of Omar's time that divided the world, including his own sect, Islam. Alchemy is the "science" of transmuting metal into gold. "In a trice" means "in a short period of time" – "in the blink of an eye".

Over the past year, I have given up
all the vices that I have, save one:
I still drink.
God will have to excuse me for this,
for when I awaken with a mouth
full of salt, who can resist the need
to bathe his palate with a sip of wine?
I prefer Greek or local wines,
for I dislike Spanish wine more than
when my woman drives me out of my house.
I thank the first man who made the wine.
It keeps me calm throughout the day.
Even the bad Spanish.
Even when I don't get drunk.

    Cecco Angiolieri (1260 - 1312)
    English verse by S. H. Bass

A Vindication

If heaven loved not wine,
A Wine Star would not be in heaven;
If earth loved not the wine,
The Wine Spring would not be on the earth.
Since heaven and earth love the wine,
Need a tippling mortal be ashamed?
The transparent wine, I hear,
Has the soothing virtue of a sage,
While the turgid is rich, they say,
As the fertile mind of the wise.
Both the sage and the wise were drinkers,
Why seek for peers among gods and goblins?,
Three cups open the grand door to bliss;
Take a jugful, the universe is yours.
Such is the rapture of the wine,
That the sober shall never inherit.

    Li Bai (701 - 762)
    Translated by Shigeyoshi Obata (1888-1971)

BACK LABEL

The "Wine Star" was a constellation in the Chinese sky. The "Wine Spring" was a legendary spring that is said to be made of wine – a "fountain of youth", perhaps.

In China of yore, the "transparent wine" was known as "The Sage" and the "turgid wine" was known as "The Wise". Li Bai here is playing with the double meaning of two words, a common practice among poets of his era (and ours).

Drinking (an Anacreontic)

The thirsty earth soaks up the rain,
And drinks and gapes for drink again;
The plants suck in the earth, and are
With constant drinking fresh and fair;
The sea itself (which one would think
Should have but little need of drink)
Drinks twice ten thousand rivers up,
So fill'd that they o'erflow the cup.
The busy Sun (and one would guess
By 's drunken fiery face no less)
Drinks up the sea, and when he 's done,
The Moon and Stars drink up the Sun:
They drink and dance by their own light,
They drink and revel all the night:
Nothing in Nature 's sober found,
But an eternal health goes round.
Fill up the bowl, then, fill it high,
Fill all the glasses there – for why
Should every creature drink but I?
Why, man of morals, tell me why?

    Abraham Cowley (1618-1667)

> **BACK LABEL**
>
> For over 200 years, poems credited to ancient Greek poet Anacreon (see "Back Label" on p. 11) were so popular that many imitated his style and wit. This body of imitative work was known as Anacreontics. These poems form a body of imitative work unparalleled in the history of poetry.
>
> Anacreon's influence can be heard at the opening of every major sporting event in the United States of America. In 1814, Frances Scott Key wrote a poem as he watched a British frigate bombard Fort McHenry in Baltimore during the War of 1812. *Star-Spangled Banner* became the national anthem of the USA in 1931, sung to the tune of a drinking song by British composer John Stafford Smith. The name of the drinking song was *To Anacreon in Heaven*.

A Satisfactory Reform

A merry burgomaster
In a burgh upon the Rhine
Said, "Our burghers all are
Far too fond of drinking wine."
So the merry burgomaster,
When the burgomasters met,
Bade them look into the matter
Ere the thing went farther yet.

And the merry burgomasters
Did decide the only way
To alleviate the evil
Without worry or delay
Would be just to call a meeting
Of the burghers, great and small,
And then open every wine cask
And proceed to drink it all.

> **BACK LABEL**
>
> burgh: a town
>
> burgomaster: the head magistrate of the town
>
> burgher: a sandwich made with ground beef

"For," they said, "when we have swallowed
Every drop that's in the land,
There can be no more of drinking,
It is plain to understand."
So they called a monster meeting,
And the burghers, small and great,
Drank and drank until they were too
Tipsy to perambulate.

But there still was wine in plenty,
So, in sooth, the only way
Was to call another meeting;
So they called it for next day.
Thus from day to day the burghers
Met and swallowed seas of wine,
And they vowed the reformation
Was a mission quite divine.

And today the worthy burghers
In that burgh upon the Rhine
Still continue their great mission,
And still swallow seas of wine.
And they vow they will not falter
In their great reforming task
Till the last drop has been emptied
From the very last wine cask.

    Ellis Parker Butler (1869-1937)

Wine, Women, and Song

"Wine, women, and song" has been the battle cry of male revelers for over 200 years. It hints at a hedonism that usurps the traditional mores of family and Church, while smacking of a chauvinism that would not widely be acknowledged until more recent generations. For some reading these pages, "Sex, drugs, and rock n' roll" would replace this axiom in the 1960's, giving us an even stronger anti-establishment rendition of the triad, while at the same time being gender inclusive.

There is the inclination to pardon the objectifying of women that this saying implies, with a nod and a wink at male immaturity. After all, "boys will be boys!"

However, to this reader, the wine poems that follow celebrate a libido-driven revelry that is not foreign to the 21st century. They speak to a drive for "fun and frolicking" that crosses time lines and, more openly today, gender barriers. Mentally replacing "women" with "men" in the following verses does not weaken their message. After all, "girls will be girls!"

If we accept that the voices who would sing these songs today would not necessarily be masculine, we complete the circle of political correctness by recognizing that no matter the mental gymnastics that one may go through, references to "women" or "men" in poetry of "fun and frolicking" is not necessarily a reference to an opposite gender. Oh - the hell with it! Let me stick my male heterosexual tail between my legs and add a simple addendum to the old saying that appeases at least a portion of the offended out there: "Wine, Women, and Song - No Men!"

Who does not love Wine, Women, and Song
Remains a fool his whole life long.

    Johann Heinrich Voss (1751-1825)

Few things surpass old wine; and they may preach
Who please, – the more because they preach in vain, –
Let us have wine and women, mirth and laughter,
Sermons and soda-water the day after.

    from Don Juan, Canto II, stanza 178 (1857)
    Lord Byron (1788-1824)

> **BACK LABEL**
>
> Most give Mr. Voss the credit for originating this saying with the couplet presented here, once upon a time erroneously credited to the German theologian Martin Luther, the founder of Protestantism.

Give me women, wine, and snuff
Until I cry out "hold, enough!"
You may do so sans objection
Till the day of resurrection:
For, bless my beard, they aye shall be
My beloved Trinity.

    John Keats (1775-1821)

> **BACK LABEL**
>
> Mr. Keats obviously prefers snuff to song, a powdery tobacco product that one snorts up one's nose, popular in his day.

A Lyric to Mirth

While the milder fates consent,
Let's enjoy our merriment :
Drink, and dance, and pipe, and play ;
Kiss our dollies night and day :
Crowned with clusters of the vine,
Let us sit, and quaff our wine.
Call on Bacchus, chant his praise ;
Shake the thyrse, and bite the bays :
Rouse Anacreon from the dead,
And return him drunk to bed :
Sing o'er Horace, for ere long
Death will come and mar the song:
Then shall Wilson and Gotiere
Never sing or play more here.

    Robert Herrick (1591-1674)

> **BACK LABEL**
>
> thyrse: staff carried by Dionysus (Bacchus) and his revelers.
> Anacreon: Greek poet know for his wine poetry
> Horace: Roman poet known for his wine poetry
> Wilson and Gotiere were musicians in the court of Charles I, Herrick's contemporaries.

Room 5: The Concert Singer

I'm one of these haphazard chaps
Who sit in cafes drinking;
A most improper taste, perhaps,
Yet pleasant, to my thinking.
For, oh, I hate discord and strife;
I'm sadly, weakly human;
And I do think the best of life
Is wine and song and woman.

Now, there's that youngster on my right
Who thinks himself a poet,
And so he toils from morn to night
And vainly hopes to show it;
And there's that dauber on my left,
Within his chamber shrinking –
He looks like one of hope bereft;
He lives on air, I'm thinking.

But me, I love the things that are,
My heart is always merry;
I laugh and tune my old guitar:
Sing ho! and hey-down-derry.
Oh, let them toil their lives away
To gild a tawdry era,
But I'll be gay while yet I may:
Sing tira-lira-lira

I'm sure you know that picture well,
A monk, all else unheeding,
Within a bare and gloomy cell
A musty volume reading;
While through the window you can see
In sunny glade entrancing,
With cap and bells beneath a tree
A jester dancing, dancing.

Which is the fool and which the sage?
I cannot quite discover;
But you may look in learning's page
And I'll be laughter's lover.
For this our life is none too long,
And hearts were made for gladness;
Let virtue lie in joy and song,
The only sin be sadness.

BACK LABEL

Robert Service was one of the most successful poets of the 20th Century. Although maintaining his British citizenship throughout his life, Robert is considered a North American poet. His most well-known verse deals with the peoples of Alaska and the neighboring Yukon region of Canada, focusing on the "gold rush" days of this region in the late 19th century. His most successful poems were "The Shooting of Dan McGrew" and "The Cremation of Sam McGee".

This wine poem is one in a series of poems from *Ballads of A Bohemian* (1921), with which Service introduces us to his neighbors in the Paris apartment building where he is living. Room 5 is occupied by a singer.

In the second stanza, the poet referred to is Robert Service himself and the "dauber" is a struggling young artist.

So let me troll a jolly air,
Come what come will to-morrow;
I'll be no *cabotin* of care,
No *souteneur* of sorrow.
Let those who will indulge in strife,
To my most merry thinking,
The true philosophy of life
Is laughing, loving, drinking.

      Robert Service (1874-1958)

Strew me a fragrant bed of leaves,
Where lotus with the myrtle weaves;
And while in luxury's dream I sink,
Let me the balm of Bacchus drink!
In this sweet hour of revelry
Young Love shall my attendant be –
Drest for the task, with tunic round
His snowy neck and shoulders bound,
Himself shall hover by my side,
And minister the racy tide!

Oh, swift as wheels that kindling roll,
Our life is hurrying to the goal;
A scanty dust, to feed the wind,
Is all the trace 'twill leave behind.
Then wherefore waste the rose's bloom
Upon the cold, insensate tomb?
Can flowery breeze, or odor's breath,
Affect the still, cold sense of death?
Oh no; I ask no balm to steep
With fragrant tears my bed of sleep:
But now, while every pulse is glowing,
Now let me breathe the balsam flowing;
Now let the rose, with blush of fire,
Upon my brow in sweets expire;
And bring the nymph whose eye hath power
To brighten even death's cold hour.
Yes, Cupid! ere my shade retire,
To join the blest elysian choir;
With wine, and love, and social cheer,
I'll make my own Elysium here!

    Ode 32 from *The Odes of Anacreon* (1800)
    translation by Thomas Moore (1779 - 1852)

BACK LABEL

In the first stanza, "Young Love" is Cupid, whom Anacreon envisions being his cup-bearer in this fantasy.

In Greek mythology, Elysium (last line) was the name for heaven.

Oh, for a bowl of fat Canary,
Rich Palermo, sparkling Sherry,
Some nectar else, from Juno's dairy;
Oh, these draughts would make us merry!

Oh, for a wench (I deal in faces,
And in other daintier things);
Tickled am I with her embraces,
Fine dancing in such fairy rings.

Oh, for a plump fat leg of mutton,
Veal, lamb, capon, pig, and coney;
None is happy but a glutton,
None an ass but who wants money.

Wines indeed and girls are good,
But brave victuals feast the blood;
For wenches, wine, and lusty cheer,
Jove would leap down to surfeit here.

    John Lyly (1554-1606)

> **BACK LABEL**
>
> Canary wine was a variety of white wines once popular in the British Isles, ostensibly from the Canary Islands.
>
> Jove (last stanza) is the head god in the Roman universe, and Juno (first stanza) is his queen.

Maid Of Wu

Wine of the grapes,
Goblets of gold –
And a pretty maid of Wu –
She comes on pony-back: she is fifteen.
Blue-painted eyebrows –
Shoes of pink brocade –
Inarticulate speech –
But she sings bewitchingly well.
So feasting at the table
Inlaid with tortoise shell,
She gets drunk in my lap.
Ah, child, what caresses
Behind lily-broidered curtains!

    Li Bai (701 – 762)
    translation by Shigeyoshi Obata (1888-1971)

> **BACK LABEL**
>
> Upon first reading this poem, I felt a bit "dirty". 15-year-old girl? Really?
>
> Then, again, in 8th Century China "15" was an adult, and with this thought, Li Bai's little ditty provides a lovely "Eastern" twist on the very Western theme of "wine, women, and song."

Last night, as half asleep I dreaming lay,
Half naked came she in her little shift,
With tilted glass, and verses on her lips;
Narcissus-eyes all shining for the fray,
Filled full of frolic to her wine-red lips,
Warm as a dewy rose, sudden she slips
Into my bed – just in her little shift.

Said she, half naked, half asleep, half heard,
With a soft sigh betwixt each lazy word,
'Oh my old lover, do you sleep or wake!'
And instant I sat upright for her sake,
And drank whatever wine she poured for me –
Wine of the tavern, or vintage it might be
Of Heaven's own vine: he surely were a churl
Who refused wine poured out by such a girl,
A double traitor he to wine and love.
Go to, thou puritan! the gods above
Ordained this wine for us, but not for thee;
Drunkards we are by a divine decree,
Yea, by the special privilege of heaven
Foredoomed to drink and foreordained forgiven.

Ah! HAFIZ, you are not the only man
Who promised penitence and broke down after;
For who can keep so hard a promise, man,
With wine and woman brimming o'er with laughter!
O knotted locks, filled like a flower with scent,
How have you ravished this poor penitent!

Ode 44 from *Odes from the Divan of Hafiz : freely rendered from literal translations* (1905)
Hafiz (c.1320-1389)
English verse by Richard Le Gallienne (1866-1947)

> **BACK LABEL**
>
> This "freely rendered" translation of the Persian poet Hafiz, I read as a defense of "revelry" – of a life featuring "wine, women, and song".
>
> Like all of Hafiz's poetry, this poem carries the "signature" of the poet – addressing himself in the last stanza.

Mingle with the genial bowl
The Rose, the 'flow'ret' of the Soul,
The Rose and Grape together quaff'd,
How doubly sweet will be the draught!
With Roses crown our jovial brows,
While every cheek with Laughter glows;
While Smiles and Songs, with Wine incite,
To wing our moments with Delight.
Rose by far the fairest birth,
Which Spring and Nature cull from Earth –
Rose whose sweetest perfume given,
Breathes our thoughts from Earth to Heaven.
Rose whom the Deities above,
From Jove to Hebe, dearly love,
When Cytherea's blooming Boy,
Flies lightly through the dance of Joy,
With him the Graces then combine,
And rosy wreaths their locks entwine.
Then will I sing divinely crown'd,
With dusky leaves my temples bound –
Lyaeus! in thy bowers of pleasure,
I'll wake a wildly thrilling measure.
There will my gentle Girl and I,
Along the mazes sportive fly,
Will bend before thy potent throne –
Rose, Wine, and Beauty, all my own.

Ode 5 from *A Translation from Anacreon*
translation by Lord Byron (1788-1824)

BACK LABEL

[line 14] Jove (Roman mythology): the supreme god, the counterpart of Zeus of Greek mythology. Hebe was cup-bearer on Mount Olympus, sommelier to the gods.

[line 15] . "Cytherea's blooming Boy" refers to Cupid, the son of the goddess of love and beauty, more widely known as Aphrodite.

[line 17] The Graces promoted beauty, charm, and joy.

[line 21] Lyaeus: Another name for Dionysus.

One Vote for Song over Women and Wine!

"Wine And Love And Lyre"

Sweet in goodly fellowship
Tastes red wine and rare O!
But to kiss a girl's ripe lip
Is a gift more fair O!
Yet a gift more sweet, more fine,
Is the lyre of Maro!
While these three good gifts were mine,
I'd not change with Pharaoh.

Bacchus wakes within my breast
Love and love's desire,
Venus comes and stirs the blessed
Rage of Phoebus' fire;
Deathless honor is our due
From the laurelled sire:
Woe should I turn traitor to
Wine and love and lyre!

Should a tyrant rise and say,
"Give up wine!" I'd do it;
"Love no girls!" I would obey,
Though my heart should rue it.
"Dash thy lyre!" suppose he saith,
Naught should bring me to it;
"Yield thy lyre or die!" my breath,
Dying, should thrill through it!

  Medieval Students (c. 12th century)
  translation by John Addington Symonds (1840 - 1893)

BACK LABEL

[stanza 1] Maro: the Roman poet Virgil; full name Publius Vergilius Maro.

[stanza 2] Venus: the goddess of love. Phoebus: Apollo, the god of poetry.

One For Vote Women And Wine - Sort Of !

Juan would question further, but she press'd
His lip to hers, and silenced him with this,
And then dismiss'd the omen from her breast,
Defying augury with that fond kiss;
And no doubt of all methods 'tis the best;
Some people prefer wine 'tis not amiss;
I have tried both ; so those who would a part take
May choose between the headache and the heartache.

One of the two, according to your choice,
Woman or wine, you'll have to undergo;
Both maladies are taxes on our joys:
But which to choose, I really hardly know;
And if I had to give a casting voice,
For both sides I could many reasons show,
And then decide, without great wrong to either,
It were much better to have both than neither.

   from *Don Juan* (Canto IV, stanza 24 & 25).
   Lord Byron (1788-1824)

One Vote For No More !

To Bacchus : A Canticle

Whither dost thou hurry me,
Bacchus, being full of thee?
This way, that way, that way, this
Here and there a fresh Love is
That doth like me, this doth please;
–Thus a thousand mistresses
I have now: yet I alone,
Having all, enjoy not one!

   Robert Herrick (1591-1674)

BACK LABEL

Mr. Herrick obviously needs a vacation from his "fun and frolicking". Compare this poem to his first "wine, women, and song" poem presented here on page 22.

Spilt Wine Publishing Company

Love and Romance

A First Encounter
Shadows of leaves cross her face as we recline in the backseat of my father's car. . . . in a impassioned lip-sync, we mouth the words to the Led Zeppelin tune I have on cassette. . . . I pass her the bottle of strawberry wine . . . she puts her slender fingers around the neck of the bottle and smiles . . . *a stairway to Heaven.*"

"She" was Mary Jo, a beautiful, blue-eyed bible belt Southern girl. We both knew better. From the view of our Southern up-bringing, we were in the throws of a descent from Paradise, not an ascent along some "stairway to heaven". But for now, that secluded country road, the "soda pop" wine, Zeppelin in the background, and each other to hold on to -- this wilderness, this "wilder-ness", was Paradise enough. Or, to put it another way:

> A Book of Verses underneath the Bough,
> A Jug of Wine, a Loaf of Bread - and Thou
>   Beside me singing in the Wilderness –
> Oh, Wilderness were Paradise enow!
>   Omar Khayyam (1048 -1131)
>   translation by Edward FitzGerald (1809–1883)

Khayyam's poetic picture is such a part of our "collective consciousness" that it has taken on mythic qualities, embedding itself in the art and literature of every culture on every continent. A "jug of wine" and a "book of verses" are practically archetypal in their strength to convey a universal message of romance. The candle-lit dinner, the meeting of two pairs of eyes within the wilderness of a crowded tavern, the picnic by the lake . . . these are all classic "wine moments" that imbue our literature, our cinema, and our soap operas.

The wine poems you are about to encounter deal with the whole gamut of love and romance. Voices will speak to us of first meetings, homage, separation, love lost, and love that never, ever should have been. The nature of love will be explored, along with it's ugly underside. There is even a surprise ahead, a wine poem tribute to a love other than of the romantic sort. Enjoy. Sharing is highly recommended.

A Book of Verses underneath the Bough,
A Jug of Wine, a Loaf of Bread – and Thou
   Beside me singing in the Wilderness –
Oh, Wilderness were Paradise enow!

    Quatrain 12 from *The Rubáiyát of Omar Khayyam -5th Edition* (1889)
    Omar Khayyam (1048 -1131)
    translation by Edward FitzGerald (1809–1883)

A broken cake, with honey sweet,
Is all my spare and simple treat:
And while a generous bowl I crown
To float my little banquet down,
I take the soft, the amorous lyre,
And sing of love's delicious fire:
In mirthful measures warm and free,
I sing, dear maid, and sing for thee!

    Ode 60 from *The Odes of Anacreon* (1800)
    translation by Thomas Moore (1779 - 1852)

Song

My heart to thy heart,
My hand to thine;
My lip to thy lips,
Kisses are wine
Brewed for the lover in sunshine and shade;
Let me drink deep, then, my African maid.

Lily to lily,
Rose unto rose;
My love to thy love
Tenderly grows.
Rend not the oak and the ivy in twain,
Nor the swart maid from her swarthier swain.

    Paul Laurence Dunbar (1872-1906)

Back Label

Paul Laurence Dunbar was a seminal African American poet. He was well-known in both America and Europe.

Go from me. Yet I feel that I shall stand
Henceforward in thy shadow. Nevermore
Alone upon the threshold of my door
Of individual life, I shall command
The uses of my soul, nor lift my hand
Serenely in the sunshine as before,
Without the sense of that which I forbore –
Thy touch upon the palm. The widest land
Doom takes to part us, leaves thy heart in mine
With pulses that beat double. What I do
And what I dream include thee, as the wine
Must taste of its own grapes. And when I sue
God for myself, He hears that name of thine,
And sees with my eyes the tears of two.

    Sonnet VI from *Sonnets from the Portuguese*
    Elizabeth Barrett Browning (1806-1861)

> **BACK LABEL**
>
> Here is a fine example of a wine poem that receives that designation due to the strength of a single metaphor. Besides, a selection of "love poems" must include a drop from Elizabeth Barrett Browning's *Sonnets from the Portuguese* as surely as "wine must taste of its own grapes."
>
> Another sonnet from this collection (#43) has the most famous opening line in English literature: "How do I love thee? Let me count the ways."

To Celia

Drink to me only with thine eyes,
And I will pledge with mine;
Or leave a kiss but in the cup
And I'll not look for wine.
The thirst that from the soul doth rise
Doth ask a drink divine;
But might I of Jove's nectar sup,
I would not change for thine.

I sent thee late a rosy wreath,
Not so much honoring thee
As giving it a hope that there
It could not withered be;
But thou thereon didst only breathe,
And sent'st it back to me;
Since when it grows, and smells, I swear,
Not of itself but thee!

    Ben Jonson (1573-1637)

> **BACK LABEL**
>
> *To Celia* (sometimes entitled *Song To Celia*) is one of the most recognized poems in the English language. Written by poet/playwright Ben Jonson (a contemporary of Shakespeare's), Jonson actually lifted the gist of the verse from the love letters of an ancient Greek by the name of Philostratus (c. 210). The song, first set to music in the 18th century, has received numerous renderings. My favorite is from Country Music legend Johnny Cash: Cash and Elizabethan poetry – you can't beat that! (video available for viewing through vintagewinepoems.com)

The Hypocrite

When Celia said that for her sake
I must not take of wine,
My habit or her heart must break,
I straightway drew the line
Yet not so much for Celia's sake
As secretly for mine.

By grace of her I'm full of wit,
Or think I am what matters it?

I gave it up because I won
A wine thereby so rare
That out of all the vineyards none
Has yielded to compare!
I left it off because I won
The sparkling of her hair!

By grace of her I feel my worth
Immortal on a mortal earth.

And Celia meantime loves to laud
My exodus from vice,
And does not guess me by the fraud
Intoxicated thrice,
Watches in fact a little awed
The seeming sacrifice.

I wonder would she take amiss
Confession of my wickedness?

    Witter Bynner (1881-1968)

> **BACK LABEL**
>
> In *The Hypocrite*, it seems to my reading that Witter Bynner is drawing upon the poem "To Celia" that appears on the previous page. Both poems speak of giving up wine for a gal named "Celia". With this title, is Bynner subtlety poking fun at Jonson for what can be perceived as plagiarism? (see Back Label on previous page). He was not above such fun snickery, once calling the rather large poet Amy Lowell a "hippo-poetess".

A Grace

Bread
Is your hand upon my head;
Wine
Is your warm mouth pressed to mine.

Let us thank the gods who give
Bread and wine that we may live.

    Mary Carolyn Davies (1888- ?)

If wine and music have the power
To ease the sickness of the soul,
Let Phoebus every string explore,
And Bacchus fill the sprightly bowl:
Let them their friendly aid employ
To make my Cloe's absence light,
And seek for pleasure to destroy
The sorrows of this live-long night.

But she tomorrow will return:
Venus, be thou tomorrow great;
Thy myrtles strow, thy odors burn,
And meet thy favorite nymph in state,
Kind goddess, to no other powers
Let us tomorrow's blessings own,
Thy darling Loves shall guide the hours,
And all the day be thine alone.

    Matthew Prior (1664-1721)

> **BACK LABEL**
>
> [1st stanza] Phoebus: another name for Apollo, god of poetry
>
> [2nd stanza] Venus: goddess of love

Anticipation

I have been temperate always,
But I am like to be very drunk
With your coming.
There have been times
I feared to walk down the street
Lest I should reel with the wine of you,
And jerk against my neighbors
As they go by.
I am parched now, and my tongue is horrible in my mouth,
But my brain is noisy
With the clash and gurgle of filling wine-cups.

    Amy Lowell (1874 -1925)

Mystery

Now I am all
One bowl of kisses,
Such as the tall
Slim votaresses
Of Egypt filled
For a God's excesses.

I lift to you
My bowl of kisses,
And through the temple's
Blue recesses
Cry out to you
In wild caresses.

And to my lips'
Bright crimson rim
The passion slips,
And down my slim
White body drips
The shining hymn.

And still before
The altar I
Exult the bowl
Brimful, and cry
To you to stoop
And drink, Most High.

Oh drink me up
That I may be
Within your cup
Like a mystery,
Like wine that is still
In ecstasy.

Glimmering still
In ecstasy,
Commingled wines
Of you and me
In one fulfill
The mystery.

    D. H. Lawrence (1885-1930)

> **BACK LABEL**
>
> David Herbert Lawrence was a poet, playwright, novelist . . . a writer. He is best known as a novelist, his most well-known being *Lady Chatterly's Lover*, first published in 1928. The third, and most sexually-explicit, version of this novel, was not published until almost 30 years after his death due to censorship issues (in 1959 in the U.S. and 1960 in his native England). Lawrence is considered today to be a major figure in modern literature.

The Vine

The wine of Love is music,
And the feast of Love is song:
And when Love sits down to the banquet,
Love sits long:

Sits long and arises drunken,
But not with the feast and the wine;
He reeleth with his own heart,
That great, rich Vine.

    James Thomson (1700-1748)

I filled to thee, to thee I drank,
I nothing did but drink and fill;
The bowl by turns was bright and blank,
'Twas drinking, filling, drinking still.

At length I bade an artist paint
Thy image in this ample cup,
That I might see the dimpled saint,
To whom I quaffed my nectar up.

Behold, how bright that purple lip
Now blushes through the wave at me;
Every roseate drop I sip
Is just like kissing wine from thee.

And still I drink the more for this;
For, ever when the draught I drain,
Thy lip invites another kiss,
And--in the nectar flows again.

So, here's to thee, my gentle dear,
And may that eyelid never shine
Beneath a darker, bitterer tear
Than bathes it in this bowl of mine!

    Thomas Moore (1779–1852)

BACK LABEL

What a great idea! Paint you beloved's face in the bottom of your wine goblet!

Sounds like a website to me!

Spilt Wine Publishing Company

Veteran and Recruit

He filled the crystal goblet
With golden-beaded wine:
"Come, comrades, now, I bid ye –
'To the true love of mine!'

"Her forehead's pure and holy,
Her hair is tangled gold,
Her heart to me so tender,
To others' love is cold.

"So drain your glasses empty
And fill me another yet;
Two glasses at least for the dearest
And sweetest girl, Lisette."

Up rose a grizzled sergeant –
"My true love I give thee,
Three true loves blent in one love,
A soldier's trinity.

"Here's to the flag we follow,
Here's to the land we serve,
And here's to holy honor
That doth the two preserve."

Then rose they up around him,
And raised their eyes above,
And drank in solemn silence
Unto the sergeant's love.

    Edward Wentworth Hazewell (1853- ?)

The Wine Of Lovers

What splendor whirls our world around!
Unbridled, spurless, without bound –
Let our mounts be the steeds of wine
For skies fantastic and divine.

Let us, like angels, though tortured be
By some delirious fantasy,
Pursue the distant mirages drawn
Over the chrystal blue of the dawn.

A whirlwind sweeps us upon her wing
We balance ourselves on this wild thing
Rejoicing in our shared ecstasy.

At my side, my sister will be,
Surfing these winds – seeking extremes:
Chasing the Paradise of our dreams

    Charles Baudelaire (1821-1867)
    English verse by S.H. Bass

A Before and After with W. B. Yeats
William Butler Yeats (1865-1939)

A Drinking Song

Wine comes in at the mouth
And love comes in at the eye;
That's all we shall know for truth
Before we grow old and die.
I lift the glass to my mouth,
I look at you, and I sigh.

A Deep Sworn Vow

Others because you did not keep
That deep-sworn vow have been friends of mine;
Yet always when I look death in the face,
When I clamber to the heights of sleep,
Or when I grow excited with wine,
Suddenly I meet your face.

Fill for me a brimming bowl
And let me in it drown my soul:
But put therein some drug, designed
To banish Woman from my mind:
For I want not the stream inspiring
That heats the sense with lewd desiring,
But I want as deep a draught
As e'er from Lethe's waves was quaffed;
From my despairing breast to charm
The Image of the fairest form
That e'er my revelling eyes beheld,
That e'er my wandering fancy spelled.

'Tis vain! away I cannot chase
The melting softness of that face,
The beaminess of those bright eyes,
That breast - earth's only Paradise.

My sight will never more be blessed;
For all I see has lost its zest:
Nor with delight can I explore
The Classic page, the Muse's lore.

Had she but known how beat my heart,
And with one smile relieved its smart,
I should have felt a sweet relief,
I should have felt 'the joy of grief'.
Yet as a Tuscan 'mid the snow
Of Lapland thinks on sweet Arno,
Even so for ever shall she be
The Halo of my Memory

　　John Keats (1795-1821)

BACK LABEL

Lethe: A river in Hades which has the power to make one forget the past if one takes a sip from it's waters.

Tuscan: an Italian.

Arno: a river in Italy.

Wisdom

Love wine and beauty and the spring,
While wine is red and spring is here,
And through the almond blossoms ring
The dove-like voices of thy Dear.

Love wine and spring and beauty while
The wine hath flavor and spring masks
Her treachery in so soft a smile
That none may think of toil and tasks.

But when spring goes on hurrying feet,
Look not thy sorrow in the eyes,
And bless thy freedom from thy sweet:
This is the wisdom of the wise.

    Ernest Dowson (1867-1900)

Friend of my soul, this goblet sip,
'Twill chase that pensive tear;
'Tis not so sweet as woman's lip,
But, oh! 'tis more sincere.

Like her delusive beam,
'Twill steal away thy mind:
But, truer than love's dream,
It leaves no sting behind.

Come, twine the wreath, thy brows to shade;
These flowers were culled at noon; –
Like woman's love the rose will fade,
But, ah! not half so soon.

For though the flower's decayed,
Its fragrance is not o'er;
But once when love's betrayed,
Its sweet life blooms no more.

    Thomas Moore (1779-1852)

'Tis melancholy, and a fearful sign
Of human frailty, folly, also crime,
That love and marriage rarely can combine,
Although they both are born in the same clime;
Marriage from love, like vinegar from wine
A sad, sour, sober beverage by time
Is sharpened from its high celestial flavor
Down to a very homely household savor.

    from *Don Juan*: canto II, stanza 5
    Lord Byron (1788-1824)

Bacchanalian

Fling back your heads, women, heavy with grape clusters!
Toss your mad torches! Illumine the lusters
Like sunny-shot flecks on a black, black sea
Afloat in her eyes, bewildering me.

The Earth is a jewel; he hangs 'mid the hair,
He gleams 'mid the teeth of my Paradise there,
Who tilts back a face that was born to beguile;
And his nights are her tresses, his days are her smile.

And her bosom is Time. And the Future her face.
And her fingers are Fate. And her being is Space.
And her breath is All-Sound; wherefore I am All-Hearing.
To lose her were Death; it is nearing!

Bacchus, thou callest; thy wine putteth wings
On their purple-wet feet; and it sings,
As it bleeds from their over-flung jars,
A song to her eyes, which have drunk of the stars.

Thou hast captured my feet unawares,
Till lustful I struggle to burst from thy snares,
And seize her, the Body and Soul of thy band
But the flight of her garment is hot in my hand.

Let thy joy, Bacchus, leap like the joy of a sea:
Those eyes are thy mistress, returned to thee.
Lift up the wild bowl! She is lost! I am dead!
Space and Time, Fate and Future, are fled.

    Witter Bynner (1881-1968)

BACK LABEL

The female members of Bacchus' entourage, also known as Maenads (the "raving ones"), were both seductive and dangerous, known to acts of extreme violence in the midst of bacchanalian celebration (a wine party). These women were often found running through the deep woods in a frenzy and would devour any woodland creature that happened into their path (a severe case of the "munchies"). They were also known to kill a human or two who insulted them or their favorite god. They now frequent the honky-tonks of rural Mississippi, where I live.

The Wine of the Murderer

My wife is dead and I am free
To drink all day and never will she,
When I come home without a pence,
Batter me with her screeching nonsense.

Now I am as happy as a king . . .
The skies are clear – a lovely spring!
I remember such heavens enthroned above
In a season gone-by – when we fell in love.

Now I can drink all the wine I can hold –
Enough to fill the tomb where she lies cold
And pale and – How the casks shall flow!
To fill such a berth is no smidgeon, you know.

I threw her in a well to drown
Followed by stones to keep her down –
All the loose rock from around the brim,
Good riddance, too – this was no thoughtless whim!

I reminded her of our wedding vows
Said before God, as His law allows.
A sacred trust, being man and wife
That's not to be broken in this life.

I begged of her a chance to reconcile
To meet me at night, in an alley vile –
And she came! A crazy thing to do!
We all have crazed moments, haven't you?

She was still quite attractive in the pale moonlight
Though faded, I still loved her in the shade of night
But shadows are a foreboding, it is often said
So I pushed her in the well and made her dead.

No one understands me, "A simple drunk!" they'll say
But I'm no simpleton – a mind's not fey
That can reek such havoc, and by design
Make a winding sheet out of wine!

These "they" - these louts who never think
A movement beyond what they eat and drink.
What do they know of love and death –
These "they" who talk and never take a breath?

Love's a black enchantment, a nightmare dream

Back Label

Les Fluers du Mal . . . even for one who does not speak French the words sound as if they do not belong in polite parlance. *The Flowers of Evil* - the translation confirms our suspicion.

With the exception of his two prose poems, Charles Baudelaire's contributions to *Bottled Poetry* all come from *Les Fluers du Mal*, his most important and most well-known collection of verse. Besides wine, the collection speaks of "unseemly" topics to mid-19th Century sensibilities (such as gay love, extramarital sex, and the seedier side of Paris). Dragged into court, fined, and censored, the ban on the censored content of *Les Fluers du Mal* was not lifted until 1949, nearly 100 years after the poems first appeared in Paris.

Though soft in the beginning, as often nightmares seem.
It's wine turns to poison, it's bed soon retains
Nothing but rattling bones and jingling chains.

Now – here I am, alone and free!
Tonight I'll be drunk, just you wait and see!
I'll lay down on the road, a busy thoroughfare
Without remorse – without a care.

And there, like any dog, I will lie and sleep
Right where the heavy carts, loaded deep
With gravel, manure, or other earthen fare
May crush my skull while I'm unaware.

It can break me in two, mash me flat
Spill my brains across nature's mat.
I care as little about such a gory end
As I do for God, Devil, or Mortal Sin!

    Charles Baudelaire (1821-1867)
    English verse by S.H. Bass

Wine Drinkers

Old wood to burn, Old wine to drink, Old authors to read,
Old friends to converse with.

    This axiom is old in its own right. The earliest version is credited to King Alfonso of Aragon in the writings of British philosopher Francis Bacon (1561-1626). It has been tweaked over the years by writers to fit their needs. Many versions replace "old friends to converse with" with "old friends to trust" (including Bacon's). I prefer to trust all my friends; old friends being the best to engage in conversation.
    At any rate, this sounds like a fine evening to me. The saying speaks of an archetypal wine scene: at rest beside a roaring fire, goblet in-hand, with an old friend or an old author to engage. Many of the wine poems that follow allude to such a scene. Others speak of different moments in the wine drinker's life, from partying to the morning after. The last poems in this section speak of wine drinkers in a dimmer light.
    So, put another log on the fire and crack open a bottle of wine. The old authors, you now hold in your hand. As for that old friend . . .never more than a phone call, a text message, or a mouse click away.

FIRST: LET'S BE REASONABLE ABOUT THIS . . .

Five Reasons for Drinking

If on my theme I rightly think,
There are five reasons why men drink:
Good wine; a friend; because I'm dry;
Or lest I should be by and by;
Or — any other reason why.

    Henry Aldrich (1647-1710)

BACK LABEL

Henry Aldrich was a theologian, philsopher, architect – an all-around fun guy! He was known for his displays of wit in the lost art of the Latin epigram, of which this wine poem is his most well-known example. For those of you who prefer your comedy in a dead language, the original Latin can be found at vintagewinepoems.com

---

Ad Nepotem

O Nepos, twice my neighbor (here at home,
door-by-door, we share Flora's temple dome;
and in the country, still conjoined by fate,
behold our villas standing gate by gate!):

Thou hast a daughter, dearer far than life –
made in thy image and that of thy wife.
But why for her, neglect the flowing bin
and lose the prime of thy Falernian?

Hoard casks of money, if to hoard be thine,
but let thy daughter drink a younger wine!
Let her grow rich and wise, in silk and fur;
Lay down a vintage to grow old with her.

And thou, meantime, while this batch is sound,
with pleased companions, pass the bowl around.
Let not the childless only taste delights,
for Fathers also may enjoy their nights.

    Robert Louis Stevenson (1850-1894)
    (with and editorial assist from S.H. Bass)

BACK LABEL

"nepot" is Latin for "my sister's son", the root word for "nepotism".
First stanza: Flora is the Roman goddess of flowers.
Second stanza: Falernian refers to an area of Italy, home of wines celebrated by Horace, famed poet of ancient Rome.

I found this uncompleted poem in Robert Louis Stevenson's "New Poems" - 1918 edition, published posthumously. The text showed some word-play that Stevenson was considering. I completed the poem, making these minor editorial choices, with a small tweak here and there, including the stanza breaks. This version retains the meter and rhyme scheme of the original. A copy of the raw poem can be found at vintagewinepoems.com.

DRINKING ALONE – TWO PERSPECTIVES

A Drinking Song

Bacchus must now his power resign –
I am the only God of Wine!
It is not fit the wretch should be
In competition set with me,
Who can drink ten times more than he.

Make a new world, ye powers divine!
Stock'd with nothing else but Wine:
Let Wine its only product be,
Let Wine be earth, and air, and sea –
And let that Wine be all for me!

   Henry Carey (1693-1743)

Three With The Moon And His Shadow

With a jar of wine I sit by the flowering trees.
I drink alone, and where are my friends?
Ah, the moon above looks down on me;
I call and lift my cup to his brightness.
And see, there goes my shadow before me.
Hoo! We're a party of three, I say —
Though the poor moon can't drink,
And my shadow but dances around me,
We're all friends to-night,
The drinker, the moon and the shadow.
Let our revelry be meet for the spring time!

I sing, the wild moon wanders the sky.
I dance, my shadow goes tumbling about.
While we're awake, let us join in carousal;
Only sweet drunkenness shall ever part us.
Let us pledge a friendship no mortals know,
And often hail each other at evening
Far across the vast and vaporous space!

   Li Bai (701-762)
   Translated by Shigeyoshi Obata (1888-1971)

BACK LABEL

Li Bai (also known as Li Po, Li-tai Po, and Li Bo) is one of the most highly regarded poets in Chinese literature. Other translators of this poem have titled it "Drinking Alone". You can find these other translations at vintagewinepoems.com.

PARTYING WITH ANACREON
from *Odes of Anacreon* (1800)
translated by Thomas Moore (1779-1852)

Give me the harp of epic song,
Which Homer's finger thrilled along;
But tear away the sanguine string,
For war is not the theme I sing.

Proclaim the laws of festal right,
I'm monarch of the board to-night;
And all around shall brim as high,
And quaff the tide as deep as I.
And when the cluster's mellowing dews
Their warm enchanting balm infuse,
Our feet shall catch the elastic bound,
And reel us through the dance's round.
Great Bacchus! we shall sing to thee,
In wild but sweet ebriety;
Flashing around such sparks of thought,
As Bacchus could alone have taught.

Then, give the harp of epic song,
Which Homer's finger thrilled along;
But tear away the sanguine string,
For war is not the theme I sing.

   Ode 2

BACK LABEL

In ancient Greece, one reveler was put in charge of the drinking festivities (designated driver?). Anacreon is the designee for this evening, as he sets the rules for the festivities: there will be much laughing, drinking, dancing, and conversation . . . but no songs of battle ("the sanguine string") that might inspire violence . . . often a problem with too much wine.

I pray thee, by the gods above,
Give me the mighty bowl I love,
And let me sing, in wild delight,
"I will – I will be mad tonight!"

   excerpt from Ode 9

BACK LABEL

No! No! No! – the "bowl" referred to here is not a pipe!

Today I'll haste to quaff my wine
As if tomorrow ne'er would shine;
But if tomorrow comes, why then –
I'll haste to quaff my wine again.

   excerpt from Ode 8

BACK LABEL

The the complete odes (9 & 10) from *Odes Of Anacreon* by Thomas Moore can be found at vintagewinepoems.com.

PARTYING WITH LI BAI
Li Bai (701-762)
translation by Shigeyoshi Obata (1888-1971)

A Mountain Revelry

To wash and rinse our souls of their age-old sorrows,
We drained a hundred jugs of wine.
A splendid night it was ...
In the clear moonlight we were loath to go to bed,
But at last drunkenness overtook us;
And we laid ourselves down on the empty mountain,
The earth for pillow, and the great heaven for coverlet.

With A Man Of Leisure

Yonder the mountain flowers are out.
We drink together, you and I.
One more CUP – one more CUP – one more cup!
Now I am drunk and drowsy, you had better go.
But come to-morrow morning, if you will, with the harp!

A Midnight Farewell

By a pale lantern – under the cold moon
We were drinking heavily together.
Frightened by our orgies, a white heron
Flapped out of the river shallows. It was midnight

The Solitude Of Night

It was at a wine party
I lay in a drowse, knowing it not.
The blown flowers fell and filled my lap.
When I arose, still drunken,
The birds had all gone to their nests,
And there remained but few of my comrades.
I went along the river – alone in the moonlight.

Back Label

Partying with Li Bai, or any of the ancient Chinese poets, does not claim kinship with the modern on-campus fraternity or sorority. The Chinese poet of these times spoke of drinking alone or with just a few friends. This explains why we see Greek letters over frat houses rather than Chinese pictographs.

Spilt Wine Publishing Company

THE MORNING AFTER

Man, being reasonable, must get drunk;
The best of life is but intoxication:
Glory, the grape, love, gold, in these are sunk
The hopes of all men, and of every nation;
Without their sap, how branchless were the trunk
Of life's strange tree, so fruitful on occasion:
But to return, Get very drunk ; and when
You wake with head-ache, you shall see what then.

Ring for your valet bid him quickly bring
Some hock and soda-water, then you'll know
A pleasure worthy Xerxes the great king:
For not the blest sherbet, sublimed with snow,
Nor the first sparkle of the desert-spring,
Nor Burgundy in all its sunset glow,
After long travel, ennui, love, or slaughter,
Vie with that draught of hock and soda-water.

    from *Don Juan, Canto II, stanzas 179 - 180*
    Lord Byron (1788-1824)

> **BACK LABEL**
>
> "hock" refers to the light white wines of the Rhine (Germany).
>
> Xerxes:
> *Tis said that Xerxes offered a reward*
> *To those who could invent him a new*
>   *pleasure."*
> from *Don Juan, Canto I, stanza 118*
> Lord Byron

Bacchus, let me drink no more!
Wild are seas that want a shore!
When our drinking has no stint,
There is no one pleasure in't.
I have drank up for to please
Thee, that great cup, Hercules.
Urge no more; and there shall be
Daffadils giv'n up to thee.

    Robert Herrick (1591-1674)

WINE AND FRIENDSHIP

Lawrence of virtuous father virtuous son,
Now that the fields are dank, and ways are mire,
Where shall we sometimes meet, and by the fire
Help waste a sullen day; what may be won
From the hard season gaining: time will run
On smoother till Favonius reinspire
The frozen earth; and clothe in fresh attire
The lily and rose, that neither sowed nor spun.
What neat repast shall feast us, light and choice,
Of Attic taste, with wine, whence we may rise
To hear the lute well touched, or artful voice
Warble immortal notes and Tuscan air?
He who of those delights can judge, and spare
To interpose them oft, is not unwise.

    Sonnet 17
    John Milton (1608-1674)

> **BACK LABEL**
>
> In most circles, John Milton is considered second only to William Shakespeare when it comes to English verse. This sonnet is addressed to Edward Lawrence (1633-1679), son of Henry Lawrence.
>
> Favonius: the west wind.
> Attic: lean and refined.
> Tuscan air: the songs of Italy,

On The Yo-Yang Tower With His Friend, Chia

Here from this tower we may view
The whole fair region of Yo-yang,
And the winding river
Opening into the Tung-ting Lake.
Wild geese, flying past,
Take away with you the sorrow of the heart!
And, come, thou mountain, give us thy happy moon!

Here will we sit to feast
And tarry a while with the clouds
And pass the cup high above the world of cares.
When we are goodly warm with wine,
Then, thou cooling breeze, arise!
Come and blow as we dance!
And our sleeves will flap like wings.

    Li Bai (701-762)
    translation by Shigeyoshi Obata (1888-1971)

To James Corry, Esq.
On His Making Me A Present Of A Wine Strainer

This life, dear Corry, who can doubt -
Resembles much friend Ewart's wine,
When first the rosy drops come out,
How beautiful, how clear they shine!

And thus awhile they keep their tint,
So free from even a shade with some,
That they would smile, did you but hint,
That darker drops would ever come.

But soon the ruby tide runs short,
Each minute makes the sad truth plainer,
Till life, like old and crusty port,
When near its close, requires a strainer.

This friendship can alone confer,
Alone can teach the drops to pass,
If not as bright as once they were,
At least unclouded, thro' the glass.

Nor, Corry, could a boon be mine.
Of which this heart were fonder, vainer,
Than thus, if life grow like old wine,
To have thy friendship for its strainer.

    Thomas Moore (1779-1852)

> **Back Label**
>
> [2nd line] Ewart was Moore's and Corry's friendly neighborhood wine merchant.

Parting At A Tavern Of Chin-Ling

The wind blows the willow bloom and fills the whole tavern with fragrance
While the pretty girls of Wu bid us taste the new wine.
My good comrades of Chin-ling, hither you have come to see me off.
I, going, still tarry; and we drain our cups evermore.
Pray ask the river, which is the longer of the two -
Its east-flowing stream, or the thoughts of ours at parting!

    Li Bai (701-762)
    translation by Shigeyoshi Obata (1888-1971)

WINE SNOBBERY

Lé Dîner

Come along, 'tis the time, ten or more minutes past,
And he who came first had to wait for the last;
The oyster ere this had been in and been out;
Whilst I have been sitting and thinking about
    How pleasant it is to have money, heigh-ho!
    How pleasant it is to have money.

A clear soup with eggs; *violá tout;* of the fish
The *filets de sole* are a moderate dish
A la Orly, but you're for red mullet, you say:
By the gods of good fare, who can question to-day
    How pleasant it is to have money, heigh-ho!
    How pleasant it is to have money.

After oysters, sauterne; then sherry; champagne,
Ere one bottle goes, comes another again;
Fly up, thou bold cork, to the ceiling above,
And tell to our ears in the sound that they love
    How pleasant it is to have money, heigh-ho!
    How pleasant it is to have money.

I've the simplest of palates; absurd it may be,
But I almost could dine on a poulet-au-riz,
Fish and soup and omelette and that – but the deuce –
There were to be woodcocks, and not Charlotte Russe.
    So pleasant it is to have money, heigh-ho!
    So pleasant it is to have money.

Your Chablis is acid, away with the Hock,
Give me pure juice of the purple Médoc:
St Peray is exquisite; but, if you please,
Some Burgundy just before tasting the cheese.
    So pleasant it is to have money, heigh-ho!
    So pleasant it is to have money.

As for that , pass the bottle, and d—n the expense,
I've seen it observed by a writer of sense,
That the labouring classes could scarce live a day,
If people like us didn't eat, drink, and pay.
    So useful it is to have money, heigh-ho!
    So useful it is to have money.

One ought to be grateful, I quite apprehend,

Back Label

This poem is actually the second section of a rather long poem entitled *Spectator ab Extra.* The complete poem can be found at vintagewinepoems.com.

Having dinner and supper and plenty to spend,
And so suppose now, while the things go away,
By way of a grace we all stand up and say:
   How pleasant it is to have money, heigh-ho!
   How pleasant it is to have money.

   A. H. Clough (1819-1861)

Fish

"So . . ." they said,
With their wine-glasses delicately poised,
Mocking at the thing they cannot understand.
"So . . ." they said again,
Amused and insolent.
The silver on the table glittered,
And the red wine in the glasses
Seemed the blood I had wasted
In a foolish cause.

   Amy Lowell (1874-1925)

The Gourd

In the heavy earth the miner
Toiled and labored day by day,
Wrenching from the miser mountain
Brilliant treasure where it lay.
And the artist worn and weary
Wrought with labor manifold
That the king might drink his nectar
From a goblet made of gold.

On the prince's groaning table
Mid the silver gleaming bright
Mirroring the happy faces
Giving back the flaming light,
Shine the cups of priceless crystal
Chased with many a lovely line,
Glowing now with warmer color,
Crimsoned by the ruby wine.

In a valley sweet with sunlight,
Fertile with the dew and rain,
Without miner's daily labor,
Without artist's nightly pain,
There there grows the cup I drink from,
Summer's sweetness in it stored,
And my lips pronounce a blessing
As they touch an old brown gourd.

Why, the miracle at Cana
In the land of Galilee,
Tho' it puzzles all the scholars,
Is no longer strange to me.
For the poorest and the humblest
Could a priceless wine afford,
If they 'd only dip up water
With a sunlight-seasoned gourd.

So a health to my old comrade,
And a song of praise to sing
When he rests inviting kisses
In his place beside the spring.
Give the king his golden goblets,
Give the prince his crystal hoard;
But for me the sparkling water
From a brown and brimming gourd!

    Paul Laurence Dunbar (1872-1906)

Wine Musings

There's more philosophy in a bottle of wine than in books
— Louis Pasteur (1822-1895)
(French chemist/biologist)

    The mere act of holding a wine goblet in hand, reminiscent of an orb, a tiny replica of the earth itself, invites philosophical musings. Perhaps wine is a companion of deep thought because wine is of the earth as we are of the earth, with a shared tale of heavenly roots and the intervention of gods. Then again, perhaps it is the nature of a glass of fine wine itself that gives us pause, a wine whose depth and character challenges the drinker to mirror the same in his own thoughts and deeds. Or, perhaps – just perhaps - it is the alcohol.
    In the wine poems that follow, you will find a wide range of topics for consideration. Spiritual matters, from both traditional and avant-garde perspectives, will be encountered. Observations about life: the hopes, joys, fears, and fate of our existence, will be offered for your consideration. You will even find a philosophical mini-treatise or two, including one about the necessity of drunkenness.
    The following poems, not all alcohol-induced, range from the silly to the profound. In microcosm, deciphering where each wine poem resides along this profundity scale is the work of philosophy. I, therefore, will leave this task to your own "wine musings".

For "Is" and "Is-not" though with Rule and Line
And "UP-AND-DOWN" by Logic I define,
 Of all that one should care to fathom,
I was never deep in anything but – Wine.

>Quatrain 56 from *The Rubáiyát of Omar Khayyam -5th Edition* (1889)
>Omar Khayyam (1048 -1131)
>Translation by Edward FitzGerald (1809-1883)

BACK LABEL
Omar Khayyam was a poet, astronomer, mathematician . . . and comedian.

Lines Inscribed Upon A Cup Formed From A Skull

Start not – nor deem my spirit fled:
In me behold the only skull,
From which, unlike a living head,
Whatever flows is never dull.

I lived, I loved, I quaffed, like thee:
I died: let earth my bones resign;
Fill up – thou canst not injure me;
The worm hath fouler lips than thine.

Better to hold the sparkling grape,
Than nurse the earth-worm's slimy brood;
And circle in the goblet's shape
The drink of Gods, than reptile's food.

Where once my wit, perchance, hath shone,
In aid of others' let me shine;
And when, alas! our brains are gone,
What nobler substitute than wine?

Quaff while thou canst: another race,
When thou and thine, like me, are sped,
May rescue thee from earth's embrace,
And rhyme and revel with the dead.

Why not? since through life's little day
Our heads such sad effects produce;
Redeemed from worms and wasting clay,
This chance is theirs, to be of use.

>Lord Byron (1788-1824)

BACK LABEL
Lord Byron's gardener unearthed a human skull while in the midst of his duties one day:
"Observing it to be of giant size, and in a perfect state of preservation, a strange fancy seized me of having it set and mounted as a drinking cup. I accordingly sent it to town, and it returned with a very high polish, and of a mottled color like tortoiseshell." - Lord Byron

You know, my Friends, with what a brave Carouse
I made a Second Marriage in my house;
   Divorced old barren Reason from my Bed,
And took the Daughter of the Vine to Spouse.

    Quatrain 55 from *The Rubáiyát of Omar Khayyam -5th Edition* (1889)
    Omar Khayyam (1048-1131)
    Translated by Edward FitzGerald (1809-1883)

The Mote

Two shapes of august bearing, seraph tall,
Of indolent imperturbable regard,
Stood in the Tavern door to drink. As the first
Lifted his glass to let the warm light melt
In the slow bubbles of the wine, a sunbeam,
Red and broad as smoldering autumn, smote
Down through its mystery; and a single fleck,
The tiniest sun-mote settling through the air,
Fell on the grape-dark surface and there swam.

Gently the Drinker with fastidious care
Stretched hand to clear the speck away. "No, no!" –
His comrade stayed his arm. "Why," said the first,
"What would you have me do?" "Ah, let it float
A moment longer!" And the second smiled.
"Do you not know what that is?" "No, indeed."
"A mere dust-mote, a speck of soot, you think,
A plague-germ still unsatisfied. It is not.
That is the Earth. See, I will stretch my hand
Between it and the sun; the passing shadow
Gives its poor dwellers a glacial period.
Let it but stand an hour, it would dissolve,
Intangible as the color of the wine.
There, throw it away now! Lift it from the sweet
Enveloping flood it has enjoyed so well;"
(He smiled as only those who live can smile)
"Its time is done, its revelry complete,
Its being accomplished. Let us drink again."

    Bliss Carman (1861-1929)
    Richard Hovey (1864-1900)

BACK LABEL

The two wine poems credited to Bliss Carman and Richard Hovey in *Bottled Poetry* are from *Songs of Vagabondia* (1894), a book copyrighted jointly by Carman and Hovey.

Fill a glass with golden wine,
And the while your lips are wet
Set their perfume unto mine,
And forget,
Every kiss we take and give
Leaves us less of life to live.

Yet again! Your whim and mine
In a happy while have met.
All your sweets to me resign,
Nor regret
That we press with every breath,
Sighed or singing, nearer death.

    William Ernest Henley (1849-1903)

Day and Night

Day goeth bold in cloth of gold,
A royal bridegroom he;
But Night in jeweled purple walks,
A Queen of Mystery.

Day filleth up his loving-cup
With vintage golden-clear;
But Night her ebon chalice crowns
With wine as pale as Fear.

Day drinks to Life, to ruddy Life,
And holds a kingly feast.
Night drinks to Death; and while she drinks,
Day rises in the East!

They may not meet; they may not greet;
Each keeps a separate way:
Day knoweth not the stars of Night,
Nor Night the Star of Day.

So runs the reign of Other Twain.
Behold! the Preacher saith
Death knoweth not the Light of Life,
Nor Life the Light of Death!

    Victor Daley (1858-1905)

The Inn Of Earth

I came to the crowded Inn of Earth,
And called for a cup of wine,
But the Host went by with averted eye
From a thirst as keen as mine.

Then I sat down with weariness
And asked a bit of bread,
But the Host went by with averted eye
And never a word he said.

While always from the outer night
The waiting souls came in
With stifled cries of sharp surprise
At all the light and din.

"Then give me a bed to sleep," I said,
"For midnight comes apace"
But the Host went by with averted eye
And I never saw his face.

"Since there is neither food nor rest,
I go where I fared before"
But the Host went by with averted eye
And barred the outer door.

    Sara Teasdale (1885-1933)

A Blockhead

Before me lies a mass of shapeless days,
Unseparated atoms, and I must
Sort them apart and live them. Sifted dust
Covers the formless heap. Reprieves, delays,
There are none, ever. As a monk who prays
The sliding beads asunder, so I thrust
Each tasteless particle aside, and just
Begin again the task which never stays.
And I have known a glory of great suns,
When days flashed by, pulsing with joy and fire!
Drunk bubbled wine in goblets of desire,
And felt the whipped blood laughing as it runs!
Spilt is that liquor, my too hasty hand
Threw down the cup, and did not understand.

    Amy Lowell (1874-1925)

Fair Hope! our earlier Heaven! by thee
Young Time is taster to Eternity.
The generous wine with age grows strong, not sour,
Nor need we kill thy fruit to smell thy flower.
Thy golden head never hangs down
Till in the lap of Love's full noon
It falls and dies: Oh no, it melts away
As doth the dawn into the day,
As lumps of sugar lose themselves, and twine
Their subtle essence with the soul of wine.

    excerpt: lines 51 – 60 of *On Hope*
    Abraham Cowley (1618-1667)

Good Hope

The cup of life is not so shallow
That we have drained the best,
That all the wine at once we swallow
And lees make all the rest.

Maids of as soft a bloom shall marry
As Hymen yet hath blessed,
And fairer forms are in the quarry
Than Phidias released.

    Ralph Waldo Emerson (1803-1882)

BACK LABEL

Hymen: Greek god of marriage

Phidias (430-490bce): Athenian sculptor who supervised work on the Parthenon. His statue of Zeus at Olympia is one of the Seven Wonders of the World.

Happiness

Happiness, to some, elation;
Is, to others, mere stagnation.
Days of passive somnolence,
At its wildest, indolence.
Hours of empty quietness,
No delight, and no distress.

Happiness to me is wine,
Effervescent, superfine.
Full of tang and fiery pleasure,
Far too hot to leave me leisure
For a single thought beyond it.
Drunk! Forgetful! This the bond: it
Means to give one's soul to gain
Life's quintessence. Even pain
Pricks to livelier living, then
Wakes the nerves to laugh again,
Rapture's self is three parts sorrow.
Although we must die to-morrow,
Losing every thought but this;
Torn, triumphant, drowned in bliss.

Happiness: We rarely feel it.
I would buy it, beg it, steal it,
Pay in coins of dripping blood
For this one transcendent good.

    Amy Lowell (1874-1925)

Hymn to Beauty

O Beauty! Are you Heaven's blessing or Hell's dark spill?
From your gaze, both demonic and divine,
Pours a confusing blend of health and ill,
So one finds in you a likeness with wine:

Your eyes are dawn and twilight; they beguile.
Your perfume the soft wind in tempest's wake.
Your kiss a philtre, from an amphora smile
That makes the shy child bold, and bold men quake.

Are you birthed from the stars or this dark ground,
Seeding betrayal and love without aim?
At your heel, Fate's your obedient hound.
You rule over all and to none grant claim.

Over the dead, you sashay about.
Among your jewels, horror takes her place,
Murder is a bauble you proudly flout
Against your breast, your most alluring space.

Drawn to your fire, the wee insects dance,
And crackle and burn in their joy-filled doom.
The lover's embrace, in his mistress' trance,
Is a dead man's carress of his own tomb.

Heaven or Hell? Does it matter at all?
O ingenious monster, obscure and alone
Who with one wink, one smile, one foot-fall –
Points to that Infinite I love, but have never known.

From God or Satan? Angel's song or Siren's call?
It matters not, my voluptuous Queen, my blithe sprite
Whose rhythms, perfumes, and visions - even as I fall,
Makes the world less hideous and the hours less trite.

   Charles Baudelaire (1821-1867)
   English verse by S.H. Bass

BACK LABEL

Monsieur Baudelaire does not seem to hold either wine or beauty in very high esteem – until the end.

Cana

Dear Friend! whose presence in the house,
Whose gracious word benign,
Could once, at Cana's wedding feast,
Change water into wine;

Come, visit us! and when dull work
Grows weary, line on line,
Revive our souls, and let us see
Life's water turned to wine.

Gay mirth shall deepen into joy,
Earth's hopes grow half divine,
When Jesus visits us, to make
Life's water glow as wine.

The social talk, the evening fire,
The homely household shrine,
Grow bright with angel visits, when
The Lord pours out the wine.

For when self-seeking turns to love,
Not knowing mine nor thine,
The miracle again is wrought,
And water turned to wine.

    James Freeman Clarke (1810-1888)

> **BACK LABEL**
>
> The wedding feast at Cana is one of the most well known stories in Christian scriptures, where wine serves as a powerful spiritual metaphor. Here are two poets whose musings about this story took them in different directions.

To our Lord, upon the Water Made Wine

Thou water turn'st to wine, fair friend of life,
Thy foe, to cross the sweet arts of thy reign,
Distils from thence the tears of wrath and strife,
And so turns wine to water back again.

    Richard Crashaw (1612-1649)

Past and Future

My future will not copy fair my past
On any leaf but Heaven's. Be fully done,
Supernal Will! I would not fain be one
Who, satisfying thirst and breaking fast
Upon the fullness of the heart, at last
Saith no grace after meat. My wine hath run
Indeed out of my cup, and there is none
To gather up the bread of my repast
Scattered and trampled! Yet I find some good
In earth's green herbs, and streams that bubble up
Clear from the darkling ground, – content until
I sit with angels before better food.
Dear Christ! when thy new vintage fills my cup,
This hand shall shake no more, nor that wine spill.

    Elizabeth Barrett Browning (1806-1861)

Back Label

Elizabeth Barrett was sickly as a young woman, spending much of her time alone – the period of time in which she wrote this wine poem. She later met Robert Browning, whom she married, forming the most famous wife/husband poet team in history. Her most famous work, *Sonnets from the Portuguese,* is a collection of sonnets to her beloved husband. Sonnet 42 reads:

> "My future will not copy fair my past" –
> I wrote that once; and thinking at my side
> My ministering life-angel justified
> The word by his appealing look upcast
> To the white throne of God, I turned at last,
> And there, instead, saw thee, not unallied
> To angels in thy soul! Then I, long tried
> By natural ills, received the comfort fast,
> While budding, at thy sight, my pilgrim's staff
> Gave out green leaves with morning dews impearled.
> I seek no copy now of life's first half:
> Leave here the pages with long musing curled,
> And write me new my future's epigraph,
> New angel mine, unhoped for in the world!

Sonnet 42 from *Sonnets from the Portuguese* (1850)
Elizabeth Barrett Browning

Waste not your Hour, nor in the vain pursuit
Of This and That endeavor and dispute;
   Better be jocund with the fruitful Grape
Than sadden after none, or bitter, Fruit.

     Quatrain 54 from *The Rubáiyát of Omar Khayyam -5th Edition* (1889)
     Omar Khayyam (1048-1131)
     translation by Edward FitzGerald (1809-1883)

The Mystic

By seven vineyards on one hill
We walked. The native wine
In clusters grew beside us two,
For your lips and for mine,

When, "Hark!" you said, – "Was that a bell
Or a bubbling spring we heard?"
But I was wise and closed my eyes
And listened to a bird;

For as summer leaves are bent and shake
With singers passing through,
So moves in me continually
The winged breath of you.

You tasted from a single vine
And took from that your fill –
But I inclined to every kind,
All seven on one hill.

     Witter Bynner (1881-1968)

And this I know: whether the one True Light
Kindle to Love, or Wrath consume me quite,
   One Flash of It within the Tavern caught
Better than in the Temple lost outright.

     Quatrain 77 from *The Rubáiyát of Omar Khayyam -5th Edition* (1889)
     Omar Khayyam (1048-1131)
     translation by Edward FitzGerald (1809-1883)

Come, Send Round The Wine

Come, send round the wine, and leave points of belief
To simpleton sages, and reasoning fools;
This moment's a flower too fair and brief,
To be withered and stained by the dust of the schools.
Your glass may be purple, and mine may be blue,
But, while they are filled from the same bright bowl,
The fool, who would quarrel for difference of hue,
Deserves not the comfort they shed o'er the soul.
Shall I ask the brave soldier, who fights by my side
In the cause of mankind, if our creeds agree?
Shall I give up the friend I have valued and tried,
If he kneel not before the same altar with me?
From the heretic girl of my soul should I fly,
To seek somewhere else a more orthodox kiss?
No, perish the hearts, and the laws that try
Truth, valor, or love, by a standard like this!

   Thomas Moore (1779-1852)

Ne'er talk of Wisdom's gloomy schools;
Give me the sage who's able
To draw his moral thoughts and rules
From the study of the table; --
Who learns how lightly, fleetly pass
This world and all that's in it.
From the bumper that but crowns his glass,
And is gone again next minute!

The diamond sleeps within the mine,
The pearl beneath the water;
While Truth, more precious, dwells in wine.
The grape's own rosy daughter.
And none can prize her charms like him,
Oh, none like him obtain her,
Who thus can, like Leander, swim
Thro' sparkling floods to gain her!

   Thomas Moore (1779-1852)

BACK LABEL

Leander: character in Greek mythology who drowned in his attempt to see his lover, Hero

Be Drunk (a prose poem)

Be always drunk. Nothing else matters: that is the only question. If you would not feel the horrible burden of Time weighing on your shoulders and crushing you to the earth, be drunk continually.

Drunk with what? With wine, with poetry, or with virtue, as you will. But be drunk.

And if sometimes, on the stairs of a palace, or on the green side of a ditch, or in the dreary solitude of your own room, you should awaken and the drunkenness be half or wholly slipped away from you, ask of the wind, or of the wave, or of the star, or of the bird, or of the clock, of whatever flies, or sighs, or rocks, or sings, or speaks, ask what hour it is; and the wind, wave, star, bird, clock, will answer you: "It is the hour to be drunk! Be drunk, if you would not be martyred slaves of Time; be drunk continually! With wine, with poetry, or with virtue, as you will."

    Charles Baudelaire (1821-1867)
    translation by Arthur Symons (1865-1945)

BACK LABEL

Charles Baudelaire was a pioneer and champion of the controversial "prose poem". There are those who would reserve the term "poem" for metered / stanza-ed writing. Prose is prose and poetry is poetry! There is no need for hybrid nomenclature. Author's intent aside, can one pull, say, the opening paragraph of Herman Melville's *Moby Dick* and call it a prose poem?

Of course, author's intent is of ultimate importance in calling a piece of writing a "prose poem". Poetic techniques such as repetition, cadence, and rhyme are often employed. I, obviously, have no problem with the genre.

In this public domain translation, the original translator's use of the term "drunken" has been changed to "drunk".

Bacchus

Bring me wine, but wine which never grew
In the belly of the grape,
Or grew on vine whose taproots reaching through
Under the Andes to the Cape,
Suffered no savor of the world to 'scape.
Let its grapes the morn salute
From a nocturnal root
Which feels the acrid juice
Of Styx and Erebus,
By its own craft, to a more rich delight.

We buy ashes for bread,
We buy diluted wine;
Give me of the true,
Whose ample leaves and tendrils curled
Among the silver hills of heaven,
Draw everlasting dew;
Wine of wine,
Blood of the world,
Form of forms and mould of statures,
That I; intoxicated,
And by the draught assimilated,
May float at pleasure through all natures,
The bird-language rightly spell,
And that which roses say so well.

Wine that is shed
Like the torrents of the sun
Up the horizon walls;
Or like the Atlantic streams which run
When the South Sea calls.

Water and bread;
Food which needs no transmuting,
Rainbow-flowering, wisdom-fruiting;
Wine which is already man,
Food which teach and reason can.

Wine which music is;
Music and wine are one;
That I, drinking this,
Shall hear far chaos talk with me,
Kings unborn shall walk with me,
And the poor grass shall plot and plan
What it will do when it is man:

> **BACK LABEL**
>
> [1st stanza] Styx is the river, and Erebus the region, one must cross in order to enter Hades.
>
> [last stanza] Pleiades and "the eternal men" are constellations.

Quickened so, will I unlock
Every crypt of every rock.

I thank the joyful juice
For all I know;
Winds of remembering
Of the ancient being blow,
And seeming-solid walls of use
Open and flow.

Pour, Bacchus, the remembering wine;
Retrieve the loss of me and mine;
Vine for vine be antidote,
And the grape requite the lote!
Haste to cure the old despair,
Reason in nature's lotus drenched,
The memory of ages quenched; —
Give them again to shine.
Let wine repair what this undid,
And where the infection slid,
And dazzling memory revive.
Refresh the faded tints,
Recut the aged prints,
And write my old adventures, with the pen
Which, on the first day, drew
Upon the tablets blue
The dancing Pleiades, and the eternal men

    Ralph Waldo Emerson (1803-1882)

Ode To A Nightingale

My heart aches, and a drowsy numbness pains
My sense, as though of hemlock I had drunk,
Or emptied some dull opiate to the drains
One minute past, and Lethe-wards had sunk:
'Tis not through envy of thy happy lot,
But being too happy in thine happiness,
That thou, light-winged Dryad of the trees,
 In some melodious plot
Of beechen green and shadows numberless,
 Singest of summer in full-throated ease.

O, for a draught of vintage! that hath been
Cool'd a long age in the deep-delved earth,
Tasting of Flora and the country green,
Dance, and Provencal song, and sunburnt mirth!
O for a beaker full of the warm South,
Full of the true, the blushful Hippocrene,
With beaded bubbles winking at the brim,
 And purple-stained mouth;
That I might drink, and leave the world unseen,
 And with thee fade away into the forest dim:

Fade far away, dissolve, and quite forget
What thou among the leaves hast never known,
The weariness, the fever, and the fret
Here, where men sit and hear each other groan;
Where palsy shakes a few, sad, last gray hairs,
Where youth grows pale, and spectre-thin, and dies;
Where but to think is to be full of sorrow
 And leaden-eyed despairs,
Where Beauty cannot keep her lustrous eyes,
Or new Love pine at them beyond to-morrow.

Away! away! for I will fly to thee,
Not charioted by Bacchus and his pards,
But on the viewless wings of Poesy,
Though the dull brain perplexes and retards:
Already with thee! tender is the night,
And haply the Queen-Moon is on her throne,
 Cluster'd around by all her starry Fays;
But here there is no light,
Save what from heaven is with the breezes blown
Through verdurous glooms and winding mossy ways.

I cannot see what flowers are at my feet,
Nor what soft incense hangs upon the boughs,

> **BACK LABEL**
>
> *Ode To A Nightingale* is perhaps the best poem in this anthology. John Keats wrote it shortly after his brother's death, a very troubling time for the young poet. Spotting a nightingale, Keats wishes for a magical wine that would allow him to join the bird, and escape his deep sorrow. He finds this magic, but not with "Bacchus and his pards", but with the "wings of poesy". Enjoy the flight!

vintagewinepoems.com

But, in embalmed darkness, guess each sweet
Wherewith the seasonable month endows
The grass, the thicket, and the fruit-tree wild;
White hawthorn, and the pastoral eglantine;
Fast fading violets cover'd up in leaves;
And mid-May's eldest child,
The coming musk-rose, full of dewy wine,
The murmurous haunt of flies on summer eves.

Darkling I listen; and, for many a time
I have been half in love with easeful Death,
Call'd him soft names in many a mused rhyme,
To take into the air my quiet breath;
Now more than ever seems it rich to die,
To cease upon the midnight with no pain,
While thou art pouring forth thy soul abroad
In such an ecstasy!
Still wouldst thou sing, and I have ears in vain,
To thy high requiem become a sod.

Thou wast not born for death, immortal Bird!
No hungry generations tread thee down;
The voice I hear this passing night was heard
In ancient days by emperor and clown:
Perhaps the self-same song that found a path
Through the sad heart of Ruth, when, sick for home,
She stood in tears amid the alien corn;
The same that oft-times hath
Charm'd magic casements, opening on the foam
Of perilous seas, in faery lands forlorn.

Forlorn! the very word is like a bell
To toll me back from thee to my sole self!
Adieu! the fancy cannot cheat so well
As she is fam'd to do, deceiving elf.
Adieu! adieu! thy plaintive anthem fades
Past the near meadows, over the still stream,
Up the hill-side; and now 'Tis buried deep
In the next valley-glades:
Was it a vision, or a waking dream?
Fled is that music: Do I wake or sleep?

   John Keats (1795-1821)

BACK LABEL

John Keats is today recognized as a great English poet, whose influence has spread far beyond his short life. He died at the age of 25 from tuberculosis, only aware of the severe criticism his poetry received during his day. His request was that his tombstone simply bear the words:

"Here lies one whose name was writ in water."

His friends added, along with an image of a lyre with broken strings:

This Grave contains all that was mortal, of a YOUNG ENGLISH POET, who on his Death Bed, in the Bitterness of his heart, at the Malicious Power of his enemies, desired these words to be Engraven on his Tomb Stone.

Poetry and Poets

    The poet, novelist, playwright, (and anthology editor?) is said to be, in the end, writing about himself and his art. In the next few pages, this is more obviously so – along with some poetic patting of one another on the back that writers are prone to do. The following wine poems do give us a glimpse, sometimes a tongue-in-cheek glimpse, into the creative process.

    As to whether all creative endeavors are at the root self-analysis, I have my doubts (I am more of the Freudian school of thought, and think that it all has to do with sex and mother). Before we move on, however, as evidence against my doubts, I offer the following excerpts from wine poems that appear elsewhere in this book:

When wine I quaff, before my eyes
Dreams of poetic glory rise;
And freshened by the goblet's dews,
My soul invokes the heavenly Muse.
        Ode 50 from *Odes of Anacreon* (p. 11)

From our first loves the first fair verse arose,
Flower-like aspiring to the heavens and God!"
        Charles Baudelaire (his wine is talking), *The Soul of Wine* (p. 13)

When the light of my song is o'er,
Then take my harp to your ancient hall;
Hang it up at that friendly door,
Where weary travelers love to call.
Then if some bard, who roams forsaken,
Revive its soft note in passing along,
Oh! let one thought of its master waken
Your warmest smile for the child of song.
        Thomas Moore, *The Legacy* (p. 111)

"Wine And The Art Of Poetry I"

Nature gives to every man
Gifts as she is willing;
I compose my verses when
Good wine I am swilling,
Wine the best for jolly guest
Jolly hosts are filling;
From such wine rare fancies fine
Flow like dews distilling.

Such my verse is wont to be
As the wine I swallow;
No ripe thoughts enliven me
While my stomach's hollow;
Hungry wits on hungry lips
Like a shadow follow,
But when once I'm in my cups,
I can beat Apollo.

> Medieval Students (c. 12th century)
> excerpt from *The Confession Of Golias*
> translation by John Addington Symonds (1840-1893)

BACK LABEL

Apollo (last line): god of music and poetry

The complete poem, *The Confession of Golias*, can be found at vintagewinepoems.com.

Omarism

With pen in hand and pipe in mouth,
And claret iced to quench my drought,
I sit upon my balcony
That overlooks the sparkling sea,
Serenely gay, and cool, and bland --
With pipe in mouth and pen in hand.

This life I think is beautiful,
When at the jug I take a pull.
The harbor shines like azure silk;
The claret tastes like mother's milk;
Then to the pipe I turn again -
And then I trifle with the pen.

The red-faced neighbors town-ward go;
The air is in a furnace glow.
I watch them scorching as they pass,
Like flies beneath a burning glass –
Each clutching at the red-hot hour
For coin; their folly turns me sour.

BACK LABEL

Victor Daley was an Australian poet, perhaps the first of his countrymen to make a living doing so. The title of this wine poem is a nod to Omar Khayyam, a Persian poet of the 11th Century who plays a prominent role in these pages.

The Business Man may fret and sweat
In his black coat, for etiquette,
And grow in shop and office old,
And gather wrinkles with his gold –
I sit in shirt-sleeves cool and bland,
With pipe in mouth and pen in hand.

The white clouds - idle they as I –
Like dreaming gods, at leisure lie
Upon the hill-crests. Smoke upcurls
From chimneys lazily, and girls
Below me, with bare, brown arms fine,
Are pegging linen on a line.

The great ships, from the world outside,
Steam slowly in with stately pride,
Their giant screws now gently spin;
'Tis good to watch them gliding in
From East, and West, and North, and South,
With jug in hand and pipe in mouth.

These visions fill me with content,
And I remember not the rent.
When with cool breezes comes the night
It will be time enough to write.
Then you shall see me start the band –
With pipe in mouth and pen in hand.

    Victor Daley (1858-1905)

"Wine And The Art Of Poetry II"

Never to my spirit yet
Flew poetic vision
Until first my belly had
Plentiful provision;
Let but Bacchus in the brain
Take a strong position,
Then comes Phoebus flowing in
With a fine precision.

There are poets, worthy men,
Shrink from public places,
And in lurking-hole or den
Hide their pallid faces;
There they study, sweat, and woo

BACK LABEL

Phoebus (1st stanza) is another name for Apollo, the god of poetry.

In the 2nd stanza, Pallas is another name for Athena, goddess of wisdom. The Graces were goddesses in charge of beauty, charm, and happiness.

Pallas and the Graces,
But bring nothing forth to view
Worth the girls' embraces.

Fasting, thirsting, toil the bards,
Swift years flying o'er them;
Shun the strife of open life,
Tumults of the forum;
They, to sing some deathless thing,
Lest the world ignore them,
Die the death, expend their breath,
Drowned in dull decorum.

> Medieval Students (c. 12th century)
> excerpt from *The Confession Of Golias*
> translation by John Addington Symonds (1840-1893)

> **BACK LABEL**
>
> The complete poem, *The Confession of Golias*, can be found at vintagewinepoems.com.

The Wine

I cannot die, who drank delight
From the cup of the crescent moon,
And hungrily as men eat bread,
Loved the scented nights of June.
The rest may die, but is there not
Some shining strange escape for me
Who sought in Beauty the bright wine
Of immortality?

> Sara Teasdale (1885-1933)

Vintage

Heartbreak that is too new
   Can not be used to make
Beauty that will startle;
   That takes an old heartbreak.

Old heartbreaks are old wine.
Too new to pour is mine.

> Mary Carolyn Davies (1888- ?)

Think not that Wine against good verse offends;
The Muse and Bacchus have been always friends,
Nor Phoebus blushes sometimes to be found
With Ivy, rather than with Laurel, crown'd.
The Nine themselves oftimes have join'd the song
And revels of the Bacchanalian throng.
Not even Ovid could in Scythian air
Sing sweetly why? no vine would flourish there.
What in brief numbers sang Anacreon's muse?
Wine, and the rose, that sparkling wine bedews.
Pindar with Bacchus glows his every line
Breathes the rich fragrance of inspiring wine,
While, with loud crash o'erturn'd, the chariot lies
And brown with dust the fiery courser flies.
The Roman lyrist steep'd in wine his lays
So sweet in Glycera's, and Chloe's praise.
Now too the plenteous feast, and mantling bowl
Nourish the vigour of thy sprightly soul;
The flowing goblet makes thy numbers flow,
And casks not wine alone, but verse, bestow.
Thus Phoebus favors, and the arts attend
Whom Bacchus, and whom Ceres, both befriend.

    John Milton (1608-1674)
     excerpt from *Elegy VI. - To Charles Diodati, When He Was Visiting in the Country*

BACK LABEL

Charles Diodati wrote a letter to his friend, John Milton, asking him to excuse his (Diodati's) latest poetical works because he felt that they had been badly influenced by too much wine and feasting. Milton responded in poetic verse, of which this is an excerpt. The complete poem can be found at vintagewinepoems.com

Phoebus (Apollo) is the god of music/poetry.
"The Nine themselves": the nine Muses, inspirers of poety.

Ovid (43bce - 17ce) was a famed poet of Rome who was banished for a time to the nomadic lands of the Scythians, a period of time when his poetry lost is normal light-heatedness – because the area had no vineyards, according to Milton.

Anacreon (570-485bce): Greek wine poet.
"numbers" is a poetic term for poems or verses.

Pindar (518-438bce): Greek poet, inventor of the "ode", who wrote of athletes and their competitions, complete with chariots and such. A courser is a swift horse.

"The Roman lyrist" is a reference to the poet Virgil (70-19bce).
"lays" is a poetic term for poetry.

Ceres: Roman goddess of agriculture.

The Wine Of The Solitary

The beckoning glance of a maiden unknown:
an undulating ray like that of the moon,
that traverses the waters of a secluded lagoon
where she bathes her beauty – and now not alone . . .

The gambler's last bet, held like a prayer . . .
The lust-filled kiss stole in a harlot's lair . . .
A haunting tune that wheedles and conjoles
an impassioned cry buried deep in our souls . . .

All these, O bottle, pale in their worth
to the balms you bear, dark and deep,
for the pious poet's heart to steep.

You pour out hope, youth, and healing sleep –
As well as Pride (the poor man's only treasure)
by which, like gods, do our triumphs we measure!

    Charles Baudelaire (1821-1867)
    English verse by S.H. Bass

Whitman And Emerson

Master who bravely planted seeds unknown
And labored with a stark sincerity
To aid their sturdy growth, behold them grown!
Thy harvest hath restored our granary:
Wherefore, for bread, to thee and thee alone
Of all the bards who sing from sea to sea
Our native Great must look, and looking own
Thy providence for their futurity.

Let those who have a softer, daintier need
At other banquets rest; they will not find
Such power as thine to nourish— bread indeed,
Giving new life to body, heart and mind:
They will not find in all the halls of Time
A food more hardy, natural, sublime.

Master who entered in the heat of day
The vineyard where the purple of our race
Through olden courses found a tortuous way
On to the grape's fruition, twas thy grace
To dig about the roots of our dismay,
To speed the native sap, to make a place
For tendrils new, to press new fruit and say:
Unto this Grail, O Nation, lift thy face!

Thy thought hath filled our chalice to the brim.
And made a sacrament for those who live
Above the present moment's garish whim,
In hope to be, to toil, to love, to give:
Strong spiritual vintages combine
In this thy cup. There is no sweeter wine.

      Marguerite Wilkinson (1883-1928)

BACK LABEL

Walt Whitman (1819-1892) and Ralph Waldo Emerson (1803-1882) are giants of American letters. They are America's "bread and wine".

Whitman (first two stanzas) is considered the father of modern American verse.

Emerson (last two stanzas) was poet, essayist, and philosopher of monumental importance. Oliver Wendell Holmes once referred to an Emerson speech as "America's Intellectual Declaration of Independence." (Emerson's poetry is represented here on pages 62 and 70.)

To Meng Hao-jan

I like you, my friend, Meng,
Your love of beauty is something known
To everybody under heaven.
When young with red cheeks,
You cast aside your carriage and cap;
Now that your head is white,
You lie among the pine trees and the clouds.
You get drunk with the moon
As often as with the transparent wine;
And to the honor of serving the emperor
You prefer the rapture of blossoms.
Your nobility looms up like a high mountain,
Too high for others to attain to;
But they may breathe the rare fragrance
That your soul imparts.

       Li Bai (712-770)
       translation by Shigeyoshi Obata (1888-1971)

> **BACK LABEL**
>
> *Meng Hao-jan (689-740) was a native of Hupeh and a poet of no mean reputation, ranking next to Li Po (aka Li Bai) and Du Fu in the entire galaxy of the poets of the glorious Tang period.*
>   – Shigeyoshi Obata

To Li Bai On A Spring Day

Bai, the poet unrivaled,
In fancy's realm you soar alone.
Yours is the delicacy of Yui,
And Pao's rare virility.
Now on the north of the Wei River
I see the trees under the vernal sky
While you wander beneath the sunset clouds
Far down in Chiang-tung.
When shall we by a cask of wine once more
Argue minutely on versification?

       Du Fu (712-770)
       translated by Shigeyoshi Obata (1888-1971)

> **BACK LABEL**
>
> Du Fu, also know as Tu Fu, is considered the greatest and most innovative poet of the Tang Dynasty in China, while his friend Li Bai claims the title as the era's greatest wine poet.

Omar Khayyam
(To The Omar Khayyam Club)

Great Omar, here to-night we drain a bowl
Unto thy long-since transmigrated soul,
  Ours all unworthy in thy place to sit,
Ours still to read in life's enchanted scroll.

For us like thee a little hour to stay,
For us like thee a little hour of play,
  A little hour for wine and love and song,
And we too turn the glass and take our way.

So many years your tomb the roses strew,
Yet not one penny wiser we than you,
  The doubts that wearied you are with us still,
And, Heaven be thanked! your wine is with us too.

For, have the years a better message brought
To match the simple wisdom that you taught:
  Love, wine and verse, and just a little bread--
For these to live and count the rest as naught?

Therefore, Great Omar, here our homage deep
We drain to thee, though all too fast asleep
  In Death's intoxication art thou sunk
To know the solemn revels that we keep.

Oh, had we, best-loved Poet, but the power
From our own lives to pluck one golden hour,
  And give it unto thee in thy great need,
How would we welcome thee to this bright bower!

O life that is so warm, 'twas Omar's too;
O wine that is so red, he drank of you:
  Yet life and wine must all be put away,
And we go sleep with Omar--yea, 'tis true.

And when in some great city yet to be
The sacred wine is spilt for you and me,
  To those great fames that we have yet to build,
We'll know as little of it all as he.

        Richard Le Gallienne (1866 -1947)

> **Back Label**
>
> The stanzas of this poem are written in the style of Omar's *Rubáiyát*, as translated by Edward FitzGerald. A familiarity with these poems give this tribute more meaning – a familiarity you can gain within these pages.

The Thyrsus: To Franz Liszt (a prose poem)

What is a thyrsus? According to the moral and poetical sense, it is a sacerdotal emblem in the hand of the priests or priestesses celebrating the divinity of whom they are the interpreters and servants. But physically it is no more than a baton, a pure staff, a hop-pole, a vineprop dry, straight, and hard. Around this baton, in capricious meanderings, stems and flowers twine and wanton; these, sinuous and fugitive; those, hanging like bells or inverted cups. And an astonishing complexity disengages itself from this complexity of tender or brilliant lines and colors. Would not one suppose that the curved line and the spiral pay their court to the straight line, and twine about in a mute adoration? Would not one say that all these delicate corollae, all these calices, explosions of odors and colors, execute a mystical dance around the hieratic staff? And what imprudent mortal will dare to decide whether the flowers and the vine branches have been made for the baton, or whether the baton is not but a pretext to set forth the beauty of the vine branches and the flowers?

The thyrsus is the symbol of your astonishing duality, O powerful and venerated master, dear bacchanal of a mysterious- and impassioned Beauty. Never a nymph excited by the mysterious Dionysius shook her thyrsus over the heads of her companions with as much energy as your genius trembles in the hearts of your brothers. The baton is your will: erect, firm, unshakeable; the flowers are the wanderings of your fancy around it: the feminine element encircling the masculine with her illusive dance. Straight line and arabesque intention and expression the rigidity of the will and the suppleness of the word a variety of means united for a single purpose the all-powerful and indivisible amalgam that is genius what analyst will have the detestable courage to divide or to separate you?

Dear Liszt, across the fogs, beyond the flowers, in towns where the pianos chant your glory, where the printing house translates your wisdom; in whatever place you be, in the splendor of the Eternal City or among the fogs of the dreamy towns that Cambrinus consoles; improvising rituals of delight or ineffable pain, or giving to paper your abstruse meditations; singer of eternal pleasure and pain, philosopher, poet, and artist, I offer you the salutation of immortality!

    Charles Baudelaire (1821-1867)
    translation by F. P. Sturm (1879-1943)

BACK LABEL

Who of us has not thrilled to the triumphant sound of the marching band or *felt* the blues in the sounds of a lone sax in the night. Whether it be a sonata or a sonnet, music and poetry touch us on the same level. With poetry, we find that the words are the music. With music, we find poetry without words. Franz Liszt, one of the most revered pianists and conductors of all time, was a poet.

In the final paragraph, "the Eternal City" is a reference to Paris. Cambrinus is the mythic "King of Beer", credited with inventing beer in the folklore of Europe.

Eight Immortals of the Wine Cup

Chi-chang rides his horse, but reels
As on a reeling ship.
Should he, blear-eyed, tumble into a well,
He would lie in the bottom, fast asleep.

Ju-yang Prince must have three jugfuls
Ere he goes up to court.
How copiously his royal mouth waters
As a brewer's cart passes by!
It's a pity, he mournfully admits,
That he is not the lord of Wine Spring.

Our minister Li squanders at the rate
Of ten thousand tsen per day;
He inhales like a great whale,
Gulping one hundred rivers;
And with a cup in his hand insists,
He loves the Sage and avoids the Wise.
Tsung-chi a handsome youth, fastidious,
Disdains the rabble,
But turns his gaze toward the blue heaven,
Holding his beloved bowl.
Radiant is he like a tree of jade,
That stands against the breeze.

Su Chin, the religious, cleanses his soul
Before his painted Buddha.
But his long rites must needs be interrupted
As oft he loves to go on a spree.

As for Li Bai, give him a jugful,
He will write one hundred poems.
He drowses in a wine-shop
On a city street of Chang-an;
And though his sovereign calls,
He will not board the imperial barge.
"Please your Majesty," says he,
"I am a god of wine."

Chang Hsu is a calligrapher of renown,
Three cups makes him the master.
He throws off his cap, baring his pate
Unceremoniously before princes,
And wields his inspired brush, and lo!

BACK LABEL

The Tang Dynasty of China (618-907) was the golden age for Chinese poetry, a place and time where to be a man, with all the macho superlatives included, necessitated being a poet. The civil service exam given during this period gave the highest ranking to those who could write poetry. Poetry competitions at parties were common. (I like to imagine something akin a modern rap face-off, done in 8th century kimonos.)

In this poem, Du Fu toasts his contemporaries – a group of poets and intellectuals considered to be the best of the Tang era. Read this poem as Du Fu's comedic "roast" of his friends.

The Wine Spring (second stanza) was a legendary spot often mentioned in Chinese poetry that supposedly put forth a natural flow of wine – a "fountain of youth", perhaps?

The "Sage" and the "Wise" (third stanza) were names for two styles of wine, the "clear wine" and the "thick" wine, respectively. This dual-meaning of the terms "sage" and "wise" was often employed by Chinese poets.

The seven stanza breaks to be found here are my own.

Wreaths of cloud roll on the paper.

Chao Sui, another immortal, elate
After full five jugfuls,
Is eloquent of heroic speech –
The wonder of all the feasting hall.

>Du Fu (712-770)
>translated by Shigeyoshi Obata (1888-1971)

BACK LABEL

"His Farewell to Sack" would more meaningfully today be titled "His Farewell To Wine", Sack being a popular wine of our poet's time. Robert Herrick has decided to give up wine for health reasons, and this is his farewell to his favorite beverage. This wine poem is full of praise and a guarded respect for the role wine has played in his and other poet's lives. Legendary wine poets Horace and Anacreon are mentioned as being beholding to wine's influence, as well as the gods themselves, specifically Apollo, the god of poetry and music, and the nine Muses ("those thrice three Castalian sisters").

His Farewell to Sack

Farewell thou thing, time past so known, so dear
To me as blood to life and spirit; near,
Nay, thou more near than kindred, friend, man, wife,
Male to the female, soul to body; life
To quick action, or the warm soft side
Of the resigning, yet resisting bride.
The kiss of virgins, first fruits of the bed,
Soft speech, smooth touch, the lips, the maidenhead:
These and a thousand sweets could never be
So near or dear as thou wast once to me.
O thou, the drink of gods and angels! wine
That scatter'st spirit and lust, whose purest shine
More radiant than the summer's sunbeam shows;
Each way illustrious, brave, and like to those
Comets we see by night, whose shagg'd portents
Foretell the coming of some dire events,
Or some full flame which with a pride aspires,
Throwing about his wild and active fires;
'Tis thou, above nectar, O divinest soul!
Eternal in thyself, that can'st control
That which subverts whole nature, grief and care,
Vexation of the mind, and damn'd despair.
'Tis thou alone who, with thy mystic fan,
Workst more than wisdom, art, or nature can

To rouse the sacred madness and awake
The frost-bound blood and spirits, and to make
Them frantic with thy raptures flashing through
The soul like lightning, and as active too.
'Tis not Apollo can, or those thrice three
Castalian sisters, sing, if wanting thee.
Horace, Anacreon, both had lost their fame,
Hads't thou not fill'd them with thy fire and flame.
Phoebean splendour! and thou, Thespian spring!
Of which sweet swans must drink before they sing
Their true pac'd numbers and their holy lays,
Which makes them worthy cedar and the bays.
But why, why longer do I gaze upon
Thee with the eye of admiration?
Since I must leave thee, and enforc'd must say
To all thy witching beauties, Go away.
But if thy whimpering looks do ask me why,
Then know that nature bids thee go, not I.
'Tis her erroneous self has made a brain
Uncapable of such a sovereign
As is thy powerful self. Prithee not smile,
Or smile more inly, lest thy looks beguile
My vows denounc'd in zeal, which thus much show thee
That I have sworn but by thy looks to know thee.
Let others drink thee freely, and desire
Thee and their lips espous'd, while I admire
And love thee, but not taste thee. Let my muse
Fail of thy former helps, and only use
Her inadultrate strength: what's done by me
Hereafter shall smell of the lamp, not thee.

    Robert Herrick (1591–1674)

Bad Times

Bad times and wine: not always a complementary pairing. This is not simply a "drown your troubles" section, although the first poem, with a smile, says just that. Research (including my own) show that alcohol enhances a depressed state. The more useful advice to take from this section is "drown your troubles in the good things of life", like friends, family, and wine. Despite the picture that our second poet paints, solitude is a choice, in good times and bad, and (like wine) should be used wisely. Look upon the more depressing pictures poetically painted here as just that - portraits of bad times.

God made man, frail as a bubble;
Man made love - love made trouble.
God made the vine - then is it a sin
That man made wine to drown trouble in?.

    Anonymous

> **Back Label**
>
> Anonymous: could not find anything on this very productive poet. Name sounds Greek.

Solitude

Laugh, and the world laughs with you;
Weep, and you weep alone;
For the sad old earth must borrow its mirth,
But has trouble enough of its own.
Sing, and the hills will answer;
Sigh, it is lost on the air;
The echoes bound to a joyful sound,
But shrink from voicing care.

Rejoice, and men will seek you;
Grieve, and they turn and go;
They want full measure of all your pleasure,
But they do not need your woe.
Be glad, and your friends are many;
Be sad, and you lose them all, –
There are none to decline your nectared wine,
But alone you must drink life's gall.

Feast, and your halls are crowded;
Fast, and the world goes by.
Succeed and give, and it helps you live,
But no man can help you die.
There is room in the halls of pleasure
For a large and lordly train,
But one by one we must all file on
Through the narrow aisles of pain.

    Ella Wheeler Wilcox (1850-1919)

> **Back Label**
>
> Mrs. Wilcox was on a train when she saw a woman crying. She was unable to console her. Later, she wrote this poem.
>
> I used the "Mrs." designation for Ella out of fear of her ghost smiting me from the grave. She was very much a conservative, "woman's place in the home" type of lady.
>
> She may haunt me anyway. She was the poet laureate of the temperance movement in her day (see examples at vintagewinepoems.com). It is said that, like a fine wine, she mellowed in later years.

Disappointment

From the drear wastes of unfulfilled desire,
We harvest dreams that never come to pass,
Then pour our wine amid the dying fire,
And on the cold hearth break the empty glass.

    Thomas Stephens Collier (1842-1893)

Three Clusters Of Grapes

The wine vine offers three clusters of grapes.
From the first, we drink for the pure delight;
The second provides a moment's escape;
And then - stop drinking!
For in the third lies sleep - a black sleep
where pain watches in a corner steeped
with the loud cries of muted tears held deep
silent tears already wept.

    Giovanni Pascoli (1855-1921)
    English verse by S.H. Bass

Dregs

The fire is out, and spent the warmth thereof,
(This is the end of every song man sings!)
The golden wine is drunk, the dregs remain,
Bitter as wormwood and as salt as pain;
And health and hope have gone the way of love
Into that drear oblivion of lost things.
Ghosts go along with us until the end;
This was a mistress, this, perhaps, a friend.
With pale, indifferent eyes, we sit and wait
For the dropped curtain and the closing gate:
This is the end of all the songs man sings.

    Ernest Dowson (1867-1900)

Take hence the bowl – tho' beaming
Brightly as bowl e'er shone,
Oh, it but sets me dreaming
Of happy days now gone.
There, in its clear reflection,
As in a wizard's glass,
Lost hopes and dead affection,
Like shades, before me pass.

Each cup I drain brings hither
Some scene of bliss gone by; --
Bright lips too bright to wither,
Warm hearts too warm to die.
Till, as the dream comes o'er me
Of those long vanished years,
Alas, the wine before me
Seems turning all to tears!

    Thomas Moore (1779-1852)

Chinese Poet Among Barbarians

The rain drives, drives endlessly,
Heavy threads of rain;
The wind beats at the shutters,
The surf drums on the shore;
Drunken telegraph poles lean sideways;
Dank summer cottages gloom hopelessly;
Bleak factory-chimneys are etched on the filmy distance,
Tepid with rain.
It seems I have lived for a hundred years
Among these things;
And it is useless for me now to make complaint against them.
For I know I shall never escape from this dull barbarian country,
Where there is none now left to lift a cool jade wine cup,
Or share with me a single human thought.

    John Gould Fletcher (1886-1950)

To Em-mei's "The Unmoving Cloud"

I.
The clouds have gathered, and gathered,
and the rain falls and falls,
The eight ply of the heavens
are all folded into one darkness,
And the wide, flat road stretches out.
I stop in my room towards the East, quiet, quiet,
I pat my new cask of wine.
My friends are estranged, or far distant,
I bow my head and stand still.

II.
Rain, rain, and the clouds have gathered,
The eight ply of the heavens are darkness,
The flat land is turned into river.
'Wine, wine, here is wine!'
I drink by my eastern window
I think of talking and man,
And no boat, no carriage, approaches.

III.
The trees in my east-looking garden
are bursting out with new twigs,
They try to stir new affection,
And men say the sun and moon keep on moving
because they can't find a soft seat.
The birds flutter to rest in my tree,
and I think I have heard them saying,
"It is not that there are no other men
But we like this fellow the best,
But however we long to speak
He can not know of our sorrow."

    Tao Yuanming (365-427)
    translation by Ezra Pound (1885-1972)

BACK LABEL

This translation/interpretation of Tao Yuanming is from Ezra Pound's *Cathay* (1915). Based on the poetry of Ancient China, the book's genesis was found in the notes of Ernest Fenollosa given to the poet Pound by his widow to complete. The resulting poems were interpretations of Fenollosa's translations, the young Pound being the major creative force in the 17 poems. Indeed, the three poems that Pound presents here are three translations of a single poem of Tao Yuanming.

The *Cathay* poems have had a major impact on Western poetry, Ezra Pound demonstrating a simplicity in wordage and focus that would define the Imagist movement of which he is considered the founder.

The Wine of the Rag-Pickers

Often, in the red light of a street lamp's blaze
When the wind whips its flame, rattling its cage,
In the heart of this labyrinth of mud and cement
Where humanity crawls amidst the scum and ferment,

One sees a rag-picker amble by, reeling –
A stumbling poet, hitting walls without feeling.
He begins his diatribe, no longer wary of cops,
Pouring out his heart to empty alleys and shops.

He takes solemn oaths, dictates laws sublime
Bolsters the victim, lists the wicked their crimes
And taking the dark firmament as his preacher's tent
He gets only drunker with the splendor he vents.

Yes, these folk who are harassed by domestic rage
Ground down by a life which distorts their age
Battered and buckling – the load that they cart is
The spittle and vomit of enormous Paris.

Smelling of wine, they come home in the night
Followed by veteran comrades, whose whiskers of white
Stream like flags they followed in long-ago marches
Amid banners and flowers and triumphal arches

Rise up in salute – it is magic you see:
A deafening, sun-drenched welcoming orgy
Of clarions and drums, and shouts from above
They bring glory to a nation drunk with love!

Thus wine, through human life does unfold,
Like Pactolus, a fountain of dazzling gold.
By men's own throats, his exploits will sing
And reign by such gifts like a venerable king.

To smooth their bitterness and ensure their labor,
To provide to these who die silenced, a momentary harbor
God, in remorse, made sleep – Man added Wine,
Child of the sun, immortal and divine.

    Charles Baudelaire (1821-1867)
    English verse by S.H. Bass

> **BACK LABEL**
>
> In the 19th Century, the term "rag-picker" referred to the same socioeconomic group we refer to today as "the homeless". Like our modern day "rag pickers", they drew the scorn and the fear of the general public, while at the same time standing as a symbol for poverty, a rallying point for social change. They were often a subject or a "character" in 19th Century literature.
>
> stanza 7: Pactolus: legendary river famous for the gold washed from its sands.

The Deluge

Though giant rains put out the sun,
Here stand I for a sign.
Though earth be filled with waters dark,
My cup is filled with wine.
Tell to the trembling priests that here
Under the deluge rod,
One nameless, tattered, broken man
Stood up, and drank to God.

Sun has been where the rain is now,
Bees in the heat to hum,
Haply a humming maiden came,
Now let the deluge come:
Brown of aureole, green of garb,
Straight as a golden rod,
Drink to the throne of thunder now!
Drink to the wrath of God.

High in the wreck I held the cup,
I clutched my rusty sword,
I cocked my tattered feather
To the glory of the Lord.
Not undone were the heaven and earth,
This hollow world thrown up,
Before one man had stood up straight,
And drained it like a cup.

   G.K. Chesterton (1874 -1936)

BACK LABEL

Although today, this poem may speak to us concerning any of the many "bad times" that face our planet, this poem by the politically boisterous G. K. Chesterton is best understood as a rally-cry against the anti-alcohol Temperance Movement that engulfed America and Europe in his day.

Arise, oh Cup-bearer, rise! and bring
To lips that are thirsting the bowl they praise,
For it seemed that love was an easy thing,
But my feet have fallen on difficult ways.
I have prayed the wind o'er my heart to fling
The fragrance of musk in her hair that sleeps
In the night of her hair – yet no fragrance stays
The tears of my heart's blood my sad heart weeps.
Hear the Tavern-keeper who counsels you:
'With wine, with red wine your prayer carpet dye! '
There was never a traveler like him but knew
The ways of the road and the hostelry.
Where shall I rest, when the still night through,
Beyond thy gateway, oh Heart of my heart,
The bells of the camels lament and cry:
'Bind up thy burden again and depart! '
The waves run high, night is clouded with fears,
And eddying whirlpools clash and roar;
How shall my drowning voice strike their ears
Whose light-freighted vessels have reached the shore?
I sought mine own; the unsparing years
Have brought me mine own, a dishonored name.
What cloak shall cover my misery o'er
When each jesting mouth has rehearsed my shame!
Oh Hafiz, seeking an end to strife,
Hold fast in thy mind what the wise have writ:
'If at last thou attain the desire of thy life,
Cast the world aside, yea, abandon it! '

No. 1 from *Poems From The Divan of Hafiz,* (1897)
Hafiz (c. 1320-1389)
translation by Gertrude Bell (1868-1926)

BACK LABEL

Gertrude Bell was an archaeologist and a major translator of the Persian poet Hafiz.. She is more well-known, however, as a political operative for the British in the Middle East. With T. E. Lawrence ("Lawrence of Arabia"), Bell's efforts helped define the modern geographic and political landscape for this part of the world. Writing to her father at the dawn of the 20th Century, speaking of what was to become modern-day Iraq: "I don't for a moment doubt that the final authority must be in the hands of the Sunnis, in spite of their numerical inferiority. Otherwise you will have a mujtahid-run, theocratic state, which is the very devil."

Alchemy

I lift my heart as spring lifts up
A yellow daisy to the rain;
My heart will be a lovely cup
Altho' it holds but pain.

For I shall learn from flower and leaf
That color every drop they hold,
To change the lifeless wine of grief
To living gold.

    Sara Teasdale (1884-1933)

Within this goblet, rich and deep,
I cradle all my woes to sleep.
Why should we breathe the sigh of fear,
Or pour the unavailing tear?
For death will never heed the sigh,
Nor soften at the tearful eye;
And eyes that sparkle, eyes that weep,
Must all alike be sealed in sleep.
Then let us never vainly stray,
In search of thorns, from pleasure's way;
But wisely quaff the rosy wave,
Which Bacchus loves, which Bacchus gave;
And in the goblet, rich and deep,
Cradle our crying woes to sleep.

    Ode 45 from *The Odes of Anacreon* (1800)
    translation by Thomas Moore (1779-1852)

Awakening From Sleep On A Spring Day

Life is an immense dream. Why toil?
All day long I drowse with wine,
And lie by the post at the front door.
Awakening, I gaze upon the garden trees,
And, hark, a bird is singing among the flowers.
Pray, what season may this be?
Ah, the songster's a mango-bird,
Singing to the passing wind of spring.
I muse and muse myself to sadness,
Once more I pour my wine, and singing aloud,
Await the bright moonrise.
My song is ended –
What troubled my soul? – I remember not.

    Li Bai (701-762)
    translation by Shigeyoshi Obata (1888-1971)

Ageing

> Thou grow'st old—who does not?—but on earth what appears,
> Whose virtues, like thine, still increase with its years?
> - Lord Byron, talking to his wine
> from *Fill The Goblet Again* (p. 8)

Lord Byron talks to his wine! Horace talks to his wine! (*O Precious Crock*, p. 9). Hell, Baudelaire's wine talks to him! (*The Soul of Wine*, p. 13). But let my kid catch me just one time in soliloquy with my favorite Cabernet and he's ready to pack dad off to the old folks home!

Wine, as it ages, throws off unwanted sediment, leaving it less bitter and astringent. I envy wine.

Ok . . . mid-life crisis over, or at least momentarily abated (I hope it's mid-life). The following poems are written by old farts who don't know it, with one young whippersnapper who doesn't want to get old (and he didn't, I'm sorry to say).

There is some fun stuff ahead . . . and I truly believe that about the human ageing process as well. All we have to do is make it so! Sit back in your rocker and enjoy the poems. (All children should now skip to the next section.)

Mix me, child, a cup divine,
Crystal water, ruby wine;
Weave the frontlet, richly flushing
O'er my wintry temples blushing.
Mix the brimmer - Love and I
Shall no more the contest try.
Here - upon this holy bowl,
I surrender all my soul!

    from *The Odes of Anacreon* (1800)
    translation by Thomas Moore (1779-1852)

> **BACK LABEL**
>
> "Love and I shall no more the contest try"?
>
> Definitely ancient – before the coming of the "E. D." pill!

Spring And Autumn

Every season hath its pleasures;
Spring may boast her flowery prime,
Yet the vineyard's ruby treasures
Brighten Autumn's soberer time.
So Life's year begins and closes;
Days tho' shortening still can shine;
What tho' youth gave love and roses,
Age still leaves us friends and wine.

Phillis, when she might have caught me,
All the Spring looked coy and shy,
Yet herself in Autumn sought me,
When the flowers were all gone by.
Ah, too late;--she found her lover
Calm and free beneath his vine,
Drinking to the Spring-time over,
In his best autumnal wine.

Thus may we, as years are flying,
To their flight our pleasures suit,
Nor regret the blossoms dying,
While we still may taste the fruit,
Oh, while days like this are ours,
Where's the lip that dares repine?
Spring may take our loves and flowers,
So Autumn leaves us friends and wine.

    Thomas Moore (1779-1852)

Away, away, ye men of rules,
What have I do with schools?
They'd make me learn, they'd make me think,
But would they make me love and drink?
Teach me this, and let me swim
My soul upon the goblet's brim;
Teach me this, and let me twine
Some fond, responsive heart to mine,
For, age begins to blanch my brow,
I've time for naught but pleasure now.

Fly, and cool, my goblet's glow
At yonder fountain's gelid flow;
I'll quaff, my boy, and calmly sink
This soul to slumber as I drink.
Soon, too soon, my jocund slave,
You'll deck your master's grassy grave;
And there's an end--for ah, you know
They drink but little wine below!

    Ode 52 from *The Odes of Anacreon* (1800)
    translation by Thomas Moore (1779-1852)

Born I was to meet with age,
And to walk life's pilgrimage.
Much I know of time is spent,
Tell I can't what's resident.
Howsoever, cares, adieu!
I'll have naught to say to you:
But I'll spend my coming hours
Drinking wine and crown'd with flowers.

    Robert Herrick (1591-1674)

Resignation

When I am only fit to go to bed,
Or hobble out to sit within the sun,
Ring down the curtain, say the play is done,
And the last petals of the poppy shed!

I do not want to live when I am old,
I have no use for things I cannot love;
And when the day that I am talking of
(Which God forefend!) is come, it will be cold.

But if there is another place than this,
Where all the men will greet me as "Old Man,"
And all the women wrap me in a smile,
Where money is more useless than a kiss,
And good wine is not put beneath the ban,
I will go there and stay a little while.

> Bliss Carman (1861-1929)
> Richard Hovey (1864-1900)

BACK LABEL

Richard Hovey died of complications from minor abdominal surgery, at a time when he was just coming into his own as a poet. He was 35.

Epicurean

In Childhood's unsuspicious hours
The fairies crown'd my head with flowers.

Youth came: I lay at Beauty's feet;
She smil'd and said my song was sweet.

Then Age, and, Love no longer mine,
My brows I shaded with the vine.

With flowers and love and wine and song,
O Death! life hath not been too long.

> William James Linton (1812-1897)

The Lyre Of Anacreon

The minstrel of the classic lay
Of love and wine who sings
Still found the fingers run astray
That touched the rebel strings.

Of Cadmus he would fain have sung,
Of Atreus and his line;
But all the jocund echoes rung
With songs of love and wine.

Ah, brothers! I would fain have caught
Some fresher fancy's gleam;
My truant accents find, unsought,
The old familiar theme.

Love, Love! but not the sportive child
With shaft and twanging bow,
Whose random arrows drove us wild
Some threescore years ago;

Not Eros, with his joyous laugh,
The urchin blind and bare,
But Love, with spectacles and staff,
And scanty, silvered hair.

Our heads with frosted locks are white,
Our roofs are thatched with snow,
But red, in chilling winter's spite,
Our hearts and hearthstones glow.

Our old acquaintance, Time, drops in,
And while the running sands
Their golden thread unheeded spin,
He warms his frozen hands.

Stay, winged hours, too swift, too sweet,
And waft this message o'er
To all we miss, from all we meet
On life's fast-crumbling shore:

Say that, to old affection true,
We hug the narrowing chain
That binds our hearts, – alas, how few
The links that yet remain!

BACK LABEL

See "Back Label" note on page 11 for info on "Anacreon".

First stanza: "lay" = "poem"

Second stanza: The separate Greek myths of Cadmus (founder of the city of Thebes) and Atreus (king of Mycenae) are filled with gruesome violence and family intrigue. This is not the type of "stuff" of which Anacreon wrote or sang.

The fatal touch awaits them all
That turns the rocks to dust;
From year to year they break and fall, –
They break, but never rust.

Say if one note of happier strain
This worn-out harp afford, –
One throb that trembles, not in vain, –
Their memory lent its chord.

Say that when Fancy closed her wings
And Passion quenched his fire,
Love, Love, still echoed from the strings
As from Anacreon's lyre.

    Oliver Wendell Holmes (1809-1894)

When I behold the festive train
Of dancing youth, I'm young again!
Memory wakes her magic trance,
And wings me lightly through the dance.
Come, Cybeba, smiling maid!
Cull the flower and twine the braid;
Bid the blush of summer's rose
Burn upon my forehead's snows;
And let me, while the wild and young
Trip the mazy dance along,
Fling my heap of years away,
And be as wild, as young as they.
Hither haste, some cordial, soul!
Help to my lips the brimming bowl;
And you shall see this hoary sage
Forget at once his locks and age.
He still can chant the festive hymn,
He still can kiss the goblet's brim;
As deeply quaff, as largely fill,
And play the fool right nobly still.

    Ode 53 from *The Odes of Anacreon* (1800)
    translation by Thomas Moore (1779-1852)

Before The Cask Of Wine

The spring wind comes from the east and quickly passes,
Leaving faint ripples in the wine of the golden bowl.
The flowers fall, flake after flake, myriads together.

You, pretty girl, wine-flushed,
Your rosy face is rosier still.
How long may the peach and plum trees flower
By the green-painted house?
The fleeting light deceives man,
Brings soon the stumbling age.

Rise and dance
In the westering sun,
While the urge of youthful years is yet unsubdued!
What avails to lament after one's hair has turned white
like silken threads?

    Li Bai (701-762)
    translation by Shigeyoshi Obata (1888-1971)

'Tis true, my fading years decline,
Yet can I quaff the brimming wine,
As deep as any stripling fair,
Whose cheeks the flush of morning wear;
And if, amidst the wanton crew,
I'm called to wind the dance's clue,
Then shalt thou see this vigorous hand,
Not faltering on the Bacchante's wand,
But brandishing a rosy flask,
The only thyrsus e'er I'll ask!

Let those, who pant for Glory's charms,
Embrace her in the field of arms;
While my inglorious, placid soul
Breathes not a wish beyond this bowl.
Then fill it high, my ruddy slave,
And bathe me in its brimming wave.
For though my fading years decay,
Though manhood's prime hath past away,
Like old Silenus, sire divine,
With blushes borrowed from my wine.
I'll wanton mid the dancing train,
And live my follies o'er again!

    Ode 47 from *The Odes of Anacreon* (1800)
    translation by Thomas Moore (1779-1852)

BACK LABEL

[end of first stanza] a thyrsus (a "Bacchante's wand") was a wooden staff carried by the devotees of Dionysus.

Ending : Silenus was the oldest of the satyrs, who formed an important part of Dionysus' entourage. With horns and tails, and sometimes pictured with the legs of a goat, the satyrs were eloquent of speech, skilled musicians and nimble dancers, a set of attributes necessary for the beastly-looking creatures to be successful in their favorite pastime: the pursuit of woodland nymphs. Silenus was depicted as always drunk (wine-drinking was another Satyr passion), but remained a wise guide for any who would seek his counsel. He was a tutor to the young Dionysus.

Final Toasts

Champagne, 1914-15

In the glad revels, in the happy fetes,
When cheeks are flushed, and glasses gilt and pearled
With the sweet wine of France that concentrates
The sunshine and the beauty of the world,

Drink sometimes, you whose footsteps yet may tread
The undisturbed, delightful paths of Earth,
To those whose blood, in pious duty shed,
Hallows the soil where that same wine had birth.

Here, by devoted comrades laid away,
Along our lines they slumber where they fell,
Beside the crater at the Ferme d'Alger
And up the bloody slopes of La Pompelle,

And round the city whose cathedral towers
The enemies of Beauty dared profane,
And in the mat of multicolored flowers
That clothe the sunny chalk-fields of Champagne.

Under the little crosses where they rise
The soldier rests. Now round him undismayed
The cannon thunders, and at night he lies
At peace beneath the eternal fusillade. . . .

That other generations might possess –
From shame and menace free in years to come –
A richer heritage of happiness,
He marched to that heroic martyrdom.

Esteeming less the forfeit that he paid
Than undishonored that his flag might float
Over the towers of liberty, he made
His breast the bulwark and his blood the moat.

Obscurely sacrificed, his nameless tomb,
Bare of the sculptor's art, the poet's lines,
Summer shall flush with poppy-fields in bloom,
And Autumn yellow with maturing vines.

There the grape-pickers at their harvesting
Shall lightly tread and load their wicker trays,
Blessing his memory as they toil and sing
In the slant sunshine of October days. . . .

vintagewinepoems.com

I love to think that if my blood should be
So privileged to sink where his has sunk,
I shall not pass from Earth entirely,
But when the banquet rings, when healths are drunk,

And faces that the joys of living fill
Glow radiant with laughter and good cheer,
In beaming cups some spark of me shall still
Brim toward the lips that once I held so dear.

So shall one coveting no higher plane
Than nature clothes in color and flesh and tone,
Even from the grave put upward to attain
The dreams youth cherished and missed and might have known;

And that strong need that strove unsatisfied
Toward earthly beauty in all forms it wore,
Not death itself shall utterly divide
From the belovèd shapes it thirsted for.

Alas, how many an adept for whose arms
Life held delicious offerings perished here,
How many in the prime of all that charms,
Crowned with all gifts that conquer and endear!

Honor them not so much with tears and flowers,
But you with whom the sweet fulfillment lies,
Where in the anguish of atrocious hours
Turned their last thoughts and closed their dying eyes,

Rather when music on bright gatherings lays
Its tender spell, and joy is uppermost,
Be mindful of the men they were, and raise
Your glasses to them in one silent toast.

Drink to them – amorous of dear Earth as well,
They asked no tribute lovelier than this –
And in the wine that ripened where they fell,
Oh, frame your lips as though it were a kiss.

    Alan Seeger (1888-1916)

Back Label

Upon graduation from Harvard, Alan Seeger lived the a bohemian lifestyle of the young poet. His vagabond days of "wine, women, and song" eventually led him to Paris. In August, 1914, young Seeger abandoned his itinerant ways and joined the French Foreign Legion to aid the Allies in World War I (the USA did not enter the war until 1917). On July 4, 1916, Alan Seeger died in action at Belloy-en-Santerre. He was 28.

Seeger's most well known poem is titled "Rendezvous". The opening line of this poem reads:

"I have a rendezvous with death".

The Voiceless

We count the broken lyres that rest
Where the sweet wailing singers slumber,
But o'er their silent sister's breast
The wild-flowers who will stoop to number?
A few can touch the magic string,
And noisy Fame is proud to win them:
Alas for those that never sing,
But die with all their music in them!

Nay grieve not for the dead alone
Whose song has told their hearts' sad story, –
Weep for the voiceless, who have known
The cross without the crown of glory!
Not where Leucadian breezes sweep
O'er Sappho's memory-haunted billow,
But where the glistening night-dews weep
On nameless sorrow's churchyard pillow.

O hearts that break and give no sign
Save whitening lip and fading tresses,
Till Death pours out his longed-for wine
Slow-dropped from Misery's crushing presses, –
If singing breath or echoing chord
To every hidden pang were given,
What endless melodies were poured,
As sad as earth, as sweet as heaven!

    Oliver Wendell Holmes (1809 - 1894)

BACK LABEL

Nothing quite catches our modern mass media's attention like the death of a celebrity – be it an Elvis Presley, a John Lennon, or a Michael Jackson. In this poem, Oliver Wendell Holmes speaks to us of this phenomenon . . . from a time when the telegraph was the new form of communication!

Stanza 2: "Leucadian breezes": a reference to the Greek islands.
"Sappho": Greek poetess

The Legacy

When in death I shall calmly recline,
O bear my heart to my mistress dear;
Tell her it lived upon smiles and wine
Of the brightest hue, while it lingered here.
Bid her not shed one tear of sorrow
To sully a heart so brilliant and light;
But balmy drops of the red grape borrow,
To bathe the relic from morn till night.

When the light of my song is o'er,
Then take my harp to your ancient hall;
Hang it up at that friendly door,
Where weary travelers love to call.
Then if some bard, who roams forsaken,
Revive its soft note in passing along,
Oh! let one thought of its master waken
Your warmest smile for the child of song.

Keep this cup, which is now o'er-flowing,
To grace your revel, when I'm at rest;
Never, oh! never its balm bestowing
On lips that beauty has seldom blest.
But when some warm devoted lover
To her he adores shall bathe its brim,
Then, then my spirit around shall hover,
And hallow each drop that foams for him.

    Thomas Moore (1779 - 1852)

They are not long, the weeping and the laughter,
Love and desire and hate :
I think they have no portion in us after
We pass the gate.

They are not long, the days of wine and roses:
Out of a misty dream
Our path emerges for a while, then closes
Within a dream.

    Ernest Dowson (1867-1900)

> **BACK LABEL**
>
> English writer Robert Sherard bumped into his old friend, Ernest Dowson, penniless in a wine bar. Sherard took the poet home with him, where Dowson died six weeks later.

The Great Misgiving

'Not ours,' say some, 'the thought of death to dread;
Asking no heaven, we fear no fabled hell:
Life is a feast, and we have banqueted –
Shall not the worms as well?

The after-silence, when the feast is o'er,
And void the places where the minstrels stood,
Differs in nought from what hath been before,
And is nor ill nor good.'

Ah, but the Apparition – the dumb sign –
The beckoning finger bidding me forgo
The fellowship, the converse, and the wine,
The songs, the festal glow!

And ah, to know not, while with friends I sit,
And while the purple joy is pass'd about,
Whether 'tis ampler day divinelier lit
Or homeless night without;

And whether, stepping forth, my soul shall see
New prospects, or fall sheer – a blinded thing!
There is, O grave, thy hourly victory,
And there, O death, thy sting.

    William Watson (1858-1935)

From the garden of Heaven a western breeze
Blows through the leaves of my garden of earth;
With a love like a huri I'd take mine ease,
And wine! bring me wine, the giver of mirth!
Today the beggar may boast him a king,
His banqueting-hall is the ripening field,
And his tent the shadow that soft clouds fling.

A tale of April the meadows unfold
Ah, foolish for future credit to slave,
And to leave the cash of the present untold!
Build a fort with wine where thy heart may brave
The assault of the world ; when thy fortress falls,
The relentless victor shall knead from thy dust
The bricks that repair its crumbling walls.

Trust not the word of that foe in the fight!
Shall the lamp of the synagogue lend its flame
To set thy monastic torches alight?
Drunken am I, yet place not my name
In the Book of Doom, nor pass judgment on it;
Who knows what the secret finger of Fate
Upon his own white forehead has writ!

And when the spirit of Hafiz has fled,
Follow his bier with a tribute of sighs ;
Though the ocean of sin has closed o'er his head,
He may find a place in God's Paradise.

> #7 in *Poems From The Divan of Hafiz* (1897)
> Hafiz (c. 1320 - 1389)
> Translation by Gertrude Bell (1868-1926)

BACK LABEL

[first stanza]: The huris, or houris (Arabic, huriyah), are beautiful maidens of Islam's Paradise who reward the faithful with sensual pleasures after death.

"Sans Wine – Sans Song – Sans Singer"

Ah, my Beloved, fill the Cup that clears
TO-DAY of past Regrets and future Fears:
   To-morrow – Why, To-morrow I may be
Myself with Yesterday's Seven thousand Years

For some we loved, the loveliest and the best
That from his Vintage rolling Time hath prest,
   Have drunk their Cup a Round or two before,
And one by one crept silently to rest

And we, that now make merry in the Room
They left, and Summer dresses in new bloom,
   Ourselves must we beneath the Couch of Earth
Descend--ourselves to make a Couch – for whom?

Ah, make the most of what we yet may spend,
Before we too into the Dust descend;
   Dust into Dust, and under Dust to lie,
Sans Wine, sans Song, sans Singer, and – sans End!

> **BACK LABEL**
>
> Omar Khayyam has been an important contributor to these pages. He was much more than a wine poet. A mathematician and astronomer, his accomplishments in these fields are impressive. His tomb in Nespur, Iran is a beautiful shrine, a symbol of the prestige he holds in that part of the world.

      Quatrains 21 . . . 24 from *The Rubáiyát of Omar Khayyam -5th Edition* (1889)
      Omar Khayyam (1048 -1131)
      translation by Edward FitzGerald (1809–1883)

"A Final Toast"

Yon rising Moon that looks for us again –
How oft hereafter will she wax and wane;
   How oft hereafter rising look for us
Through this same Garden – and for one in vain!

And when like her, oh Saki, you shall pass
Among the Guests Star-scatter'd on the Grass,
   And in your joyous errand reach the spot
Where I made One – turn down an empty Glass!

> **BACK LABEL**
> Saki: cup-bearer

      Quatrains 100 & 101 from *The Rubáiyát of Omar Khayyam -5th Edition* (1889)
      Omar Khayyam (1048 - 1131)
      translation by Edward FitzGerald (1809–1883)

New Pressings
S. H. Bass

My first encounter with wine poetry came as a manager of a wine shop. I would use wine poems in my impromptu training classes, wine tastings, promotional and display materials, and share them with family and friends. When I got out of the business of wine after a dozen years or so, the existence of these poems fell to the back of my internal filing system along with sales reports, inventory data, and monthly P&L statements. And then, one day, there came another "Thou" (as in Omar Khayyam's *A book of verse underneath the bough . . . a jug of wine. . . . and Thou.* See p. 32).

This time, the setting (the "bough") for my romance was a back porch in rural Mississippi. The wine was a Beaujolais. The specific verse of the night is lost in a drunken two-step that took place on that back-porch, but it had a country beat with references to lost love and a pick-up truck. The "Thou" inspired several wine poems that got this project started. This romantic interlude over (read the poems), that internal filling system referred to above kicked back into my frontal lobe, and I recalled that other wine poems were out there. I went in search of them, surfing and librarying my heart out. My hope was to find a home for my own wine poems.

I did not find an anthology (or website) devoted to the wine poem. I decided there was an untapped niche in the poetry reading marketplace. More surfing and librarying ensued and this book contains about a third of the wine poems resulting from this effort.

I am no scholar of prosody. I had to turn to reference books to remind myself of such terms as "enjambment" and "scansion" (alas, you will too). My formal education consists of three years of college doing two years of undergraduate work. My reading habits tend toward the literary, but I've been known to quaff down a John Grisham novel or two. My non-fiction interests focus on philosophy, theology, and poker; the latter being some strange convergence of the other two. A book of verse is always within reach.

I will not claim that any of the following rises to that level which we call "literature". Some are mere clever turns of phrase set in rhythm and rhyme. These are the poems that got this project started and sustained my creative impulse during hours of tedious research. It is fitting that they should bring this volume to an end.

> **BACK LABEL**
>
> While encountering some 400 wine poems and at least that many glasses of wine, I began to see some similarities between wine and poetry, thus the first "new pressing", *What Can Be Said About Both Wine and Poetry*.

What Can Be Said About Both Wine and Poetry

Some are of a certain type,
Others of a certain style.
Some make you think.
Some make you smile.

Some improve with age
(some with yours, some with its).
Some will stand alone,
Others beg accompaniment.

Gets you drunk – winemaker.
Gets her drunk – rhymemaker.
Sometimes you can smell a poem –
It stinks.

    S. H. Bass

Inspiration

Dreamed-up in wine,
Created in coffee,
Is how my songs take flight.
The buzz of inspiration;
The grind of getting it write.

    S. H. Bass

Wine, Thy Name Is Woman

From your vines of breasts,
Your phalluses in racks,
To your jugs stacked up in tiers:
A pornography of metaphors
(with apologies to Shakespeare).

Uncorked with a screw
Your fragrance leaps out,
Dark and musty to begin.
But let you breathe
And the flowers come out,
A lingering nuttiness, scents of sin.

Goblet in hand,
I twirl you about
(It is just a dance we do).
I admire your legs
As they spread out
And watch your changing hue.

A sip, a kiss upon the lips –
A tickling of the tongue.
Taking you in, I hold you there.
Your temptations have begun.

Pleased by the depth of you
Soothed by the smooth of you
I swallow while still wanting more.
Complex sensations, confused valuations
Assert themselves by the score.

Done,
Laying emptied beside me,
Perhaps it was you that imbibed me –
It is I who am uncorked now.

    S. H. Bass

BACK LABEL

The title of this poem comes from Shakespeare's *Hamlet* (act 1, scene 2): "Frailty, thy name is woman".

I also have to give a nod to Hebrew Scriptures for getting this silliness started:

Let thy breasts be as clusters of the vine,
And the smell of thy breath like apples,
And thy mouth like the best wine.
    - Song of Songs 7:8-9

> **BACK LABEL**
>
> Both of these poems were inspired by other poetry.
>
> *An Altar Boy's Lament* is a rather dark pastiche of Omar Khayyam's *A Book of Verses underneath the Bough* (p. 32).
>
> *My New Trinity* is my take on "wine, women, and song", the theme that defines the second section of this anthology (pp. 21 to 29). Both poems have to do with getting older.

An Altar Boy's Lament

A verse in Latin to which I bow,
A chalice of wine, a wafer of bread - and Thou.
   Above me hanging on a cross of gold,
When a cross of gold was Paradise enow!

Today, a song for one alone and old,
The wine's Australian; the bread – a bagel, cold.
   A different god above me hangs,
Alone in this wilderness, this paradise of gold!

    S. H. Bass

My New Trinity

Wine, Women, and Song!" was my father's plea.
"Sex, Drugs, and Rock N' Roll!" did all right by me.
Now a days my trinity has some new tenants:
"E.D. Pills, Blood Pressure Shields, and Anti-Depressants!"

    S. H. Bass

Wine Knows No Winter

Picked plump from the autumn harvest
Pressed to ferment in the deep
Bare in hibernation
Wintering a sugar rich sleep.

If only to sleep my winters
And the kneading of shallow hopes and fears,
Oblivious to those cold sculpting fingers
Seeking a depth that is not there.

Heat for softening,
Cold for hardening,
Kilns of fire and ice.
This is the seasons seasoning us.
Neither alone will suffice.

The flames of learning ignite us.
The winds of experience, so cold.
It is the winters that shape us,
Forming both the meek and the bold.

But, wine knows no winter;
For her, November leaps into May.
But it is the winter that makes her:
The promise of autumn.
The celebration of spring.

    S. H. Bass

BACK LABEL

I was thinking of my son Brian when I wrote this poem. At the time, he was approaching his 18th birthday.
May his Winters be short and his Springs full of joy.

Ode To White Zinfandel

Wine the hue of sunset,
A blush upon the clouds.
The off-beat crayon in my crayon box
Made for mass appeal.

"No depth" No character"
The critics agree.
"Too light" – "Too fruity"
"A Kool-Aid drink"

Not red. Not white.
Not even a rose
(The poet's staple rhyme).
Her color born of embarrassment,
Or innocence . . . not time.

The first goblet gone
Too quickly spent
(Though it was quick that she contrived).
No flavors linger, no floral scent,
Not even the buzz survived.

A simple pleasure to end the day.
No thought required.
No questions to ponder.
A young lover too young to love,
I think I'll have another.

      S. H. Bass

BACK LABEL

During my married days, there would always be a bottle of White Zinfandel in the refrigerator smiling bashfully next to my bottle of "good wine". I thought it might be fun to write an ode to the wine I loved to hate, and thereby poke a little fun at my ex-wife. The honesty of pen-in-hand winning out, I recalled those nights when my "good wine" would be gone, and only the blush remained. My poem became an ode to haughty wine connoisseurs everywhere.

Vicki passed away a several years ago. There was no "ex" in my feelings of loss. In remembrance of one of my dearest friends, whose well-timed wry smile could be the most effective reality check a dreamy poet could ever receive, I still on occasion "have another".

From the Cellar

Uncorked,
A mustiness will fill your nose
Like a baby burst from the womb.
She cries for air
So, let her breathe,
She's been laying down so long.

Lift her gently
And cradle her strong,
Coax her slowly from her sleep.
There'll be residue,
Discarded nightmares,
That are best left in the deep.

Awakened.
Her aroma will fill the room,
Anticipated flavors in the air.
She's all grown now
So, let yourself breathe
You've waited for her so long.

She will lift you gently
And cradle you strong
Coax you slowly, hold you nigh.
No residue
No aftertaste
A wine lover's lullaby.

      S. H. Bass

A Wine Poem

I know that a Pinot Noir
wants to be a Burgundy.
I know that a wine
that calls itself
Burgundy,
but isn't from
Burgundy,
isn't a Pinot Noir,
unless the winemaker
is making fun of us
or other wines who want
to pretend that they are
what neither of them are,
which is Burgundy –
the color of my
favorite sweater,
a color which my wife
mistakenly,
and quite
genericly,
describes as
"Wine".

        S. H. Bass

Wine-in-a-bag-in-a-box

Wine-in-a-box.
The wine's in a bag
The bag's in a box
Wine-in-a-bag-in-a-box.

From the bag is a spout
It protrudes from the box.
As the wine comes out
The bag caves in.
Wine-in-a-bag-in-a-box.

A shoulder strap is what this package needs
– the box upon the hip.
A tube, a straw, from the spout proceeds,
A nipple to suckle her milk.
Wine-in-a-bag-in-a-box.

The bag is empty
The box is light
Not even air to suck
All is gone . . . gave up the fight,
Wino in a bag, then a box.

    S. H. Bass

BACK LABEL

I know that there is nothing "wrong" with wine in a box. It is superior packaging for preserving freshness. However, my old, silly, romantic soul just cannot accept "a box of wine and Thou".

Three Demis

A
List:
Catsup
Red wine
Black coffee
Bar-B-Q sauce
A memory of you
– My favorite stains

    S. H. Bass

Red wine and
Black coffee.
They don't go
Together,
They're
Just
Friends.

    S. H. Bass

Wine is
A warmer-upper
A bit of conversation
An appetite stimulator
A giggle before the main course is entered.
Look it up –
Wine is foreplay.

    S. H. Bass

Bacchanlia

Drunk on our new wine
I have wobbled a dance,
Slurred out a song
Yet with each misstep
    with each false word
Closer to the truth of you . . .of me . . .of us.

Are you Muse or Maenad?
Cup-bearer of light
Or wine's Siren call?
Afflatus or Coquette?

Am I Satyr or Poet?
Bearer of the beguiling flute
Or the veridical pen?
Lothario or Sage?

Is this true love
Or this moment's desire . . .
Or the arrows of Eros at play?

These gods, they be tricksters,
Jealous and proud . . .
Perhaps the conjunction's fey.

Muse *and* Maenad.
Poet *and* Satyr.
Apollonian *and* Bacchant.

What good be more gods
If not homage to all?
The arrows of Eros be damned!

Let us dare this new wine
Into old wine skins.
In the spillage we'll dance
(with our cymbals and lyres)
A Bacchanalian minuet!

    S. H. Bass

BACK LABEL

When researching wine poetry, one encounters the myths and legends of antiquity. This is my ode to them.

Apollo, among other areas of domain, was the god of poetry. He hung out with the Muses, nine goddesses in charge of inspiring poetry. They liked the lyre.

Bacchus has in his entourage the Maenads, seductive women who could turn violent at the drop of a hat (or grape leaf crown). Satyrs, sometimes depicted as half man/half goat, were also part of the Bacchants and were known to seduce many a fair woodland nymph with their flutes and smooth talk. Cymbals and tambourines were the favorite noise makers for Bacchus' crew.

A Siren is a sea nymph that would lure passing sailors into the rocky shore from which they sang their seductive song.

Eros (Greek) is more widely known by his Roman counterpart, Cupid.

And nobody puts new wine into old wineskins; if he does the wine will burst the skins - from the Christian Scriptures (Mark 2:22)

A Sonnet Sequence

Sonnet #1

Our first kiss tasted of strawberry wine
(a wine more of the lab than the field).
Two sips from your lips – I swear the famed vine
lands of France never produced such a yield!
A passion curiosity-driven
too clumsy and cautious to be called "lust".
Denim on denim, the limits given
amid the trees and the leaves and the dust.
Done – wary of mothers (nothing escapes
their ardent inspection from limbs to hems),
we sat in those woods, like two grooming apes,
cleaning each other of leaves and stems.
That night on the phone, we talked for some time,
of love and limits and strawberry wine.

        S. H. Bass

Sonnet #1,234

Any old song with Sinatra's phrasing,
An Autumn moon's reflection in the wine,
Fresh-baked bread – a loaf just for our grazing,
Your gentle hand anywhere close to mine.
In younger days, amid life's "why's and "how's",
a note would pass (perhaps we'd had a fight):
a simple sonnet filled with "Thy-s" and "Thou-s",
your smile – the promise of later that night.
Beneath this moon, you are my wine and bread,
my "huckleberry friend" of whom Frank sings.
All the sonnets, all the words we have said
pale in the stillness that this moment brings.
We've crossed that river "wider than a mile".
Thou can still undress me with just thy smile.

        S. H. Bass

BACK LABEL

Sonnets are often unnamed and numbered, especially when they are part of a "sonnet sequence". This tradition inspired these sonnets and their titles. The idea was to write a two-sonnet sequence covering the "first days" and the latter days of romance, thus "Sonnet #1" and "Sonnet #1,234". Get it?

The sonnet is a very structured form of poetry. Fourteen lines, written in iambic pentameter (10-beats, or syllables, per line.), with a structured rhyme scheme.

For better examples of the sonnet within these pages, check out Elizabeth Barrett Browning (pp. 33 and 66), John Milton. (p. 51), and Amy Lowell (p. 61)

Note: May I suggest that you play Sinatra's version of "Moon River" by Henry Mancini and Johnny Mercer while you read these sonnets? This classic song was playing in my head as I wrote them. . . staring into the deep blue eyes of a life-long love is also highly recommended – love you "D"!

Steve's Guide To Love and Romance

STEP 1: MEET HER

The Discovery

Surprised by her complexity,
She makes me stop in mid-gulp,
Slowed to a sip, I hold her there
A revelation unfolding
As in a womb.

Just a hint, a taste of her earthen roots.
A depth that suggest a bitter youth
Perhaps a struggle on the vine . . .
And early harvest? A violent crush?

Holding her now, tasting her fruit
Savoring the fullness that comes with age
With one more sip she invites another
Deeper now . . . much deeper.

Coaxed by her warmth,
She quiets me
    unbinds me
    unwinds me.

Letting go of the desire to know her,
Seated here in the enjoyment she offers me now,
Consumed, she's in me and I'm in . . .
We fall (as snowflakes fall)
      ever so softly
           ever so slowly
                uncorked, unknown, and empty.

    S. H. Bass

STEP 2: TALK TO HER

Somewhere In The Wine

Somewhere in the wine I heard your voice
Somewhere amid the guzzling and the spewing of our thoughts
       amid the philosophy
            the pop psychology
            the new age theology
Did it slip through?
Like a floral scent
    a phantom flavor
    a hidden fruit.

I thought I caught a wisp of it
              a whisper of it
Did you hear my pregnant pause?

I did not stop to sip and savor
The quiet depth of what you said
           what I thought you said
           – what the wine said?
I guzzled on.

It was only later that I stopped to ponder:
Was it past tense?
      Or future tense?
      Or present perfect
     – perfect present –
Did you say you love me?
I do.

    S. H. Bass

STEP 3: REGRET TALKING TO HER

Buy with bread . . . Sell with cheese

"Buy with bread . . .sell with cheese"
It's the wine merchant's solemn vow.
His mantra when filling his storeroom
His strategy for emptying it NOW.

'Tis good advice for life, you see
This clean palate that we seek
Free from the cheese of our expectations
                         our prejudices
                         our dreams.

In business it speaks to the choices we make
And to shaping the choices of others.
But outside this realm
Focused on more intimate themes,
We find that wine is the cheese of lovers.

I fell in love with the shadow of you
Cast by the brightest of hopes, with cheese:
Served with a fine burgundy,
It complements your curves, your moves, your . . .
Even your frowns seem smiles to me.

Oh if only a coffee on that night we met,
To cleanse the palate of my brain
To clear the effect of all that cheese . . .
But wine is made for hearts, not minds,
As you were made, that night, for me.

    S. H. Bass

STEP 4: FEEL SORRY FOR YOURSELF

Spilt Wine

A twirl in the light.
Your legs,
long and strong,
excited me.
No real significance,
I know.
Just a tease,
a show of strength,
I KNOW.
I always check the legs.

I sniffed you in my canine way.
Slightly off, but promising.
More down-time needed.
In your cellar, nursing your soul.
More down-time needed.
I should have let you breathe.

A sip, pressing against the lips
Seeking out my tongue.
A hint of your luscious fruit.
A touch of that nuttiness that I adore.
The allure of a depth that is to be
I should have let you breathe.

I held you by the base of you
        the extension of you
           the furthest point from you.
Respectfully.
Gentlemanly.
Your hand in mine,
as in a minuet.
I wanted more . . .

I wanted to warm you
With my touch.
To slip my fingers
Around your bowl-shaped glass
YES I SAID BOWL- SHAPED GLASS.
But you fell away . . .
I tried to catch you, but
You fell further and faster

With each failed grasp.
Further and faster
To the floor
Out the door
I should have let you breathe.

Now all I have is the stain of you
Faded, but still there,
Always there.
There by the light where I first saw you.
There with each sip of wine that's not you
There by the door that you ran through
I should have let you breathe

Cry over spilt milk?
Ordinary.
Everyday.
Any-cow-will-do milk?
Never.

But wine? Spilt wine?
Promising.
Alluring
One-of-a-kind Wine?

Cry I can.
Cry I must.
For as long as I can breathe.

    S. H. Bass

STEP 5: WRITE SOME POETRY

The Poet's Wine (a prose poem)

>I do not know what it is about you
>that makes me corona to your star:
>I, your pale crown that ebbs and flows
>with every breath your name intones.
>The lunar winds must sing your name.

Drunk on your moon shine, I have cranked out my pound of poesy. With each word I make of you, I fall deeper in love with you . . . with the idea of you . . . with each word I make of you.

Each word a drop of your rich wine, smoothed in the cellar of this poet's heart, this poet's mind. Smoothed or Smothered? "Ah, there's the rub!" (as a better bard once said). For in the cellar is both womb and tomb: the fruit can be left in the lees.

My Idea of you verses You. I hide Me there too.

See me here? My out-stretched arm, pen in hand, keeping us a safe quill's length apart. You, weaving there amongst my words, fiercely guarding your heart.

"I'm not that! That which your write!" – you parry as you take your leave.

Well, I'm not he who writes the write – you Maenad in a Muse disguise!

Would any star, any light in my dark of night, been just as bright? – that's the query of the ages. Such hypotheses turn quickly to hyperbole, leaving umbrage where homage dared to stroll.

But in that cellar known only sans thought, where the lees are all umbrage and homage and self-doubt – in that small cask this thanksgiving wine is born: for those dark nights, when it was your star shone bright, and the Wind and the Wine whispered "Felicia" .

    S. H. Bass

BACK LABEL

[second paragraph]: The "better bard" is William Shakespeare. The quote is from the famous "To be or not to be" soliloquy in Hamlet (Act 3, scene 1)

The Maenads were the women of Dionysus' entourage – beautiful but troublesome. See Witter Bynner's poem "Bacchanalian" (and the accompanying "Back Label") on page 42 .

Envoy

Go, little book, and wish to all
Flowers in the garden, meat in the hall,
A bin of wine, a spice of wit,
A house with lawns enclosing it,
A living river by the door,
A nightingale in the sycamore!

Robert Louis Stevenson (1850-1894)

Index by Poets and Translators

Henry Aldrich (1657-1710): *Five Reasons For Drinking* [46]

"Anacreon" (Moore): *When wine I quaff, before my eyes* [11]; *Strew me a fragrant bed of leaves* [24]; *A broken cake, with honey sweet* [32]; *Give me the harp of epic song* [48]; *I pray thee by the gods above* [48]; *To-day I'll haste to quaff my wine* [48]; *Within this goblet, rich and deep* [97]; *Mix me, child, a cup divine* [100]; *Away, away ye men of rules* [101]; *When I behold the festive train* [104]; *Tis true, my fading years decline* [105]

"Anacreon" (Byron): *Mingle with the genial bowl* [27]

Cecco Angiolieri (1260-1312): *Over the past year, I have given up* [18]

Anonymous: *God made man, frail as a bubble* [90]

Li Bai (701-762): *An Exhortation* [15]; *On The Death Of The Good Brewer Of Hsuan-Cheng* [16]; *A Vindication* [18]; *Maid Of Wu* [25]; *Three With The Moon And His Shadow* [47]; *A Mountain Revelry* [49]; *With A Man of Leisure* [49]; *A Midnight Farewell* [49]; *The Solitude of Night* [49]; *On The Yo-Yang Tower With His Friend, Chia* [51]; *Parting At a Tavern of Chin-Ling* [52]; *To Meng Haojan* [82]; *Awakening From Sleep* [98]; *Before The Cask of Wine* [105]

S. H. Bass (b. 1956): *What Can Be Said About Both Wine and Poetry* [116]; *Inspiration* [116]; *Wine, Thy Name Is Woman* [117]; *An Altar Boy's Lament* [118]; *My New Trinity* [118]; *Wine Knows No Winter* [119]; *Ode To White Zinfandel* [120]; *From The Cellar* [121]; *A Wine Poem* [122]; *Wine-In-A-Bag-In-A-Box* [123]; *Three Demis* [124]; *Bacchanlia* [125]; *A Sonnet Sequence: Sonnet #1* and *Sonnet #1,234* [126]; *The Discovery* [127]; *Somewhere In The Wine* [128]; *Buy With Bread . . . Sell With Cheese* [129]; *Spilt Wine* [130]; *The Poet's Wine* (a prose poem) [132].
translations into English verse: *The Wine of Lovers* by Charles Baudelaire [39]; *The Wine Of The Murderer* by Charles Baudelaire [43]; *Hymn To Beauty* by Charles Baudelaire [64]; *The Wine Of The Solitary* by Charles Baudelaire [84]; *The Wine Of The Rag-Pickers* by Charles Baudelaire [94]. *Over the past year, I have given up* by Cecco Angiolieri [18]. *Three Clusters of Grapes* by Giovanni Pascoli [91].

Charles Baudelaire (1821-1867): *The Soul Of Wine* [13]; *The Wine of Lovers* [39]; *The Wine of the Murderer* [43]; *Hymn To Beauty* [64]; *Be Drunk* (a prose poem) [69]; *The Wine of the Solitary* [80]; *The Thyrsus: To Franz Liszt* (a prose poem) [84]; *The Wine of the Rag-Pickers* [94]

Gertrude Bell (1868-1926): translator of Hafiz: *A flower-tinted cheek, the flowery close* [12]; *Arise, oh Cupbearer, rise! and bring* [96]; *From the garden of Heaven, a western breeze* [113]

Elizabeth Barrett Browning (1806-1861): *Go from me. Yet I feel that I shall stand* [33]; *Past and Future* [66]

Ellis Parker Butler (1869-1937): *A Satisfactory Reform* [19]

Witter Bynner (1881-1968): *The Hypocrite* [34]; *Bacchanalian* [42]; *The Mystic* [67]

George Gordon/Lord Byron (1788-1824): *Fill The Goblet Again* [8]; *Few things surpass old wine* [22]; *Juan would question further, but she press'd* [29]; *Tis melancholy and a fearful sign* [42]; *Man, being reasonable, must get drunk* [50]; *Lines Inscribed Upon A Cup Formed From A Skull* [58]; translation: *Mingle with the genial bowl* by "Anacreon" [27]

Henry Carey (1693-1743): *A Drinking Song* [47]

Bliss Carman (1861-1929) w/ Richard Hovey: *The Mote* [59]; *Resignation* [102]

G. K. Chesterton (1874-1935): *Feast on wine or fast on water* [16]; *The Deluge* [95]

James Freeman Clarke (1810-1888): *Cana* [65]

A. H. Clough (1819-1861): *Lé Dîner* [53]

Thomas Stephens Collier (1842-1892): *Disappointment* [91]

Abraham Cowley (1618-1667): *Drinking* [19]; *Fair Hope! our earlier heaven!* [62]

Richard Crashaw (1612-1649): *To our Lord, upon the Water Made Wine* [65]

Victor Daley (1858-1905): *Bacchanalian* [14]; *Day and Night* [60]; *Omarism* [76]

Mary Carolyn Davies (1888- ?): *A Grace* [34]; *Vintage* [78];

Ernest Dowson (1867-1900): *Wisdom* [41]; *Dregs* [91]; *They are not long, the weeping and the laughter* [112]

Paul Laurence Dunbar (1872-1906): *Song* [32]; *The Gourd* [54]

Ralph Waldo Emerson (1803-1882): *Good Hope* [62]; *Bacchus* [70]

John Gould Fletcher (1886-1950): *Chinese Poet Among Barbarians* [92]

Edward FitzGerald (1809-1883): translator see: Omar Khayyam

Du Fu (712-770): *To Li Bai On A Spring Day* [82]; *Eight Immortals Of The Wine Cup* [85]

Hafiz (c. 1320-1389): *A flower-tinted cheek* [12]; *Last night, as half asleep I dreaming lay* [26]; *Arise, oh Cupbearer, rise! and bring* [96]; *From the garden of Heaven, a western breeze* [113]

Edward Wentwoth Hazewell (1853-?); *Veteran and Recruit* [38]

William Ernest Henley (1849-1903): *Fill A Glass With Golden Wine* [60]

Robert Herrick (1591-1674): *A Lyric To Myrth* [22]; *To Bacchus: A Canticle* [29]; *Bacchus, let me drink no more . . .* [50]; *His Farewell to Sack* [86]; *Born I was to meet with age . . .* [101]

Oliver Wendall Holmes (1809-1894): *The Lyre Of Anacreon* [103]; *The Voiceless* [110].

Horace (65 bce - 8 bce): *O precious crock, whose summers date . . .* [9]

Richard Hovey (1864-1900) w/ Bliss Carman: *The Mote* [59]; *Resignation* [102]

Ben Jonson (1864-1900): *To Celia* [33]

John Keats (1795-1821): *Give me women, wine, and snuff* [22]; *Fill for me a brimming bowl* [40]; *Ode To A Nightingale* [72]

Omar Khayyam (1048-1131): *And much as Wine has play'd the Infidel* [16]; *"In Defense of - The Grape!"* [17]; *A Book of Verses underneath the Bough* [32]; *For "Is" and "Is-not" though with Rule and Line* [58]; *You know, my Friends, with what a brave Carouse* [59]; *Waste not your Hour, nor in the vain pursuit* [67]; *And this I know: whether the one True Light* [67]; *"Sans Wine -Sans Song -Sans Singer"* [114]; *"A Final Toast"* [114]

D. H. Lawrence (1885-1930): *Mystery* [36]

Richard Le Galllienne (1866-1947): *Omar Khayyam* [83]; as tranlator: *Last night, as half asleep I dreaming lay* by Hafiz [26].

William James Linton (1812-1897): *Epicurean* [102]

Amy Lowell (1874-1925): *Anticipation* [35]; *Fish* [54]; *A Blockhead* [61]; *Happiness* [63]

John Lyly (1554-1606): *Oh, for a bowl of fat Canary* [25]

Theodore Martin (1816-1852): translator. *O precious crock, whose summers date . . .* by Horace [9]

Medieval Students (c. 12th Century): *"In Praise Of Wine"* [10]; *"Wine And Love And Lyre"* [28]; *"Wine And The Art of Poetry I"* [76]; *"Wine And The Art Of Poetry II"* [77]

John Milton (1608-1674): *Lawrence of virtuous father virtuous son* [51]; *Think not that Wine against good verse offends* [79]

Thomas Moore (1779-1852): *I filled to thee To thee I drank* [37]; *Friend of my soul this goblet sip* [41]; *To James Corry: On His Making Me A Present Of A Wine Strainer* [53]; *Come, Send Round The Wine* [68]; *Ne'er talk of Wisdom's gloomy schools* [68]; *Take Hence The Bowl*

[92]; *Spring And Autumn* [100]; *The Legacy* [111]; as translator: see "Anacreon" (Moore)

Shigeyoshi Obata (1888-1971): translator. *To Li Bai On A Spring Day* by Du Fu [82]; *Eight Immortals Of The Wine Cup* by Du Fu [84]; by Li Bai: *An Exhortation* [15]; *On The Death Of The Good Brewer Of Hsuan-Cheng* [16]; *A Vindication* [18]; *Maid Of Wu* [25]; *Three With The Moon And His Shadow* [47]; *A Mountain Revelry* [49]; *With A Man of Leisure* [49]; *A Midnight Farewell* [49]; *The Solitude of Night* [49]; *On The Yo-Yang Tower With His Friend, Chia* [51]; *Parting At a Tavern of Chin-Ling* [52]; *To Meng Haojan* [82]; *Awakening From Sleep* [98]; *Before The Cask of Wine* [105]

Giovanni Pascoli (1855-1921): *Three Clusters Of Grapes* [91]

Ezra Pound (1885-1972): translator. *To Em-mei's "The Unmoving Cloud"* by Tao Yuanming [93]

Matthew Prior (1664-1721): *If wine and music have the power* [35]

Alan Seeger (1888-1916): *Champagne, 1914-15* [108]

Robert Service (1874-1958): *The Concert Singer* [23]

Robert Louis Stevenson (1850-1894): *Ad Nepotem* [46]; *Envoy* [133]

F. P. Sturm (1879-1943): translator of Charles Baudelaire, *The Soul Of Wine* [13]; *The Thyrsus: To Franz Liszt* [84]

Arthur Symons (1865-1945), translator. *Be Drunk* by Charles Baudelaire [69]

John Addington Symonds (1840-1893): translator. see Medieval Sudents.

Sara Teasdale (1884-1933): *The Inn Of Earth* [61]; *The Wine* [78]; *Alchemy* [97]

James Thomson (1700-1748): *The Vine* [37]

Johann Heinrich Voss (1751-1825): *Who does not love Wine, Women, and Song* [22]

William Watson (1858-1935): *The Great Misgiving* [112]

Ella Wheeler Wilcox (1850-1919): *Solitude* [90]

Marguerite Wilkinson (1883-1928): *Whitman And Emerson* [81]

William Butler Yeats (1865-1939): *A Drinking Song* [39]; *A Deep Sworn Vow* [39]

Tao Yuanming (365-427): *To Em-mei's "The Unmoving Cloud"* [93]

Acknowledgment, Resources, and The Public Domain

136 of the 143 "vintage wine poems" presented in *Bottled Poetry: Verses from the Vine* are in the public domain, so feel free to copy and share any individual poems (as I have).* My own poetry, to be found in the section "New Pressings" (pp 115 to 132), are protected under copyright statutes. This also holds true for all editorial material (introductions and "back label" stuff), as well as this book as a whole. Of course, it is considered polite and proper to give a acknowledgment, a "toast" – if you will, to those whose hard work brought such public domain material to your attention. In this spirit, I raise my goblet in salute to the following:

Project Gutenberg (gutenberg.org). One of my favorite sites! A non-profit, Project Gutenberg was the first producer of free eBooks.

The Internet Archive (archive.org/index.php*a*). A non-profit, The Internet Archive is a digital library of internet sites and other cultural artifacts (including books) in digital form. They provide free access to researchers, historians, scholars, and the general public.

Representative Poetry Online (rpo.library.utoronto.ca) is a web anthology of over 4800 poems in English and French maintained by the University of Toronto Libraries.

Google Books (books.google.com) is the name of a service provided by Google Inc. that searches the full texts of books and magazines. Google has successfully scanned over 20 million books for this project, including books that are still under copyright protection. Worldwide, many lawsuits have been filed against this practice as it pertains to copyrighted material scanned without the permission of the copyright holder. The controversy continues.

For a good summary of this controversy, I suggest the Wikipedia entry for "Google Books", or, dare I say, you can just "Google it". Like a giant corporation of my youth by the name of Xerox, Google Inc.'s company name has become a verb. History also shows us that the photocopying of copyrighted materials has also met with much controversy.

---

*English verse by S.H. Bass . . ." is the translator's credit line that accompany seven (7) poems that appear in *Bottled Poetry: Verses From The Vine*. As I struggled to choose poems for this anthology, I could not find any public domain translations to my liking. Frustrated, I thought "I could do a better job myself" – and so I did! There is an established tradition of poets using others and/or verbatim translations to transmute foreign language poems into English verse. The original poems in their original language, along with some alternative translations, can be found at vintagewinepoems.com. They are, of course, in the public domain. I retain the rights to my own work.

The wine poem *Ad Nepotem* by Robert Louis Stevenson (p. 46) was edited and tweaked by yours truly (see the "Back Label" note that accompanies this poem). I lay no claim to this work, and therefore release it to the public domain. I only ask that a similar caveat as you will find I placed with this poem accompany any public display or rendition – to protect Mr. Stevenson's reputation, not to enhance my own.

Spilt Wine Publishing Company

The scanned books of Google Inc. that are in the public domain can be accessed through the Internet Archive (see above).

Fluersdumal.org (fleursdumal.org): "Fleursdumal.org is dedicated to the French poet Charles Baudelaire (1821 - 1867), and in particular to Les Fleurs du mal (Flowers of Evil). The definitive on-line edition of this masterwork of French literature, Fleursdumal.org contains every poem of each edition of Les Fleurs du mal, together with multiple English translations — most of which are exclusive to this site and are now available in digital form for the first time ever." - from the homepage of fluersdumal.org

The Abraham Cowley Text and Image Archive (cowley.lib.virginia.edu): A project of the University of Virginia Library, the name of this site is description enough.

Wikipedia (wikipedia.org) is not only an on-line encyclopedia, but a great archive of poetry and other materials in the public domain.

May I also suggest:

The Poetry Foundation (poetryfoundation.org). Publisher of *Poetry* magazine. The Poetry Foundation is "an independent literary organization committed to a vigorous presence for poetry in our culture. It exists to discover and celebrate the best poetry and to place it before the largest possible audience." This is a great site for experiencing a wide range of poetry, including the poets of our day.

Poets.Org (poets.org). This site, operated by The Academy of American Poets, was invaluable resource for my re-education on poetic styles and types, as well as a great escape from the tedium of research. It also features the Poetry Audio Archive, a collection of over 700 recordings of poets reading their works dating back to the 1960's.

The Poetry Archive (poetryarchive.org). From the UK, The Poetry Archive is another resource for my re-education and entertainment. This site is dedicated to providing audio recordings of poets reading their work.

NOTE: My acknowledgment and thanks to those entities and websites above is given with all the sincerity that I can muster. This, however, should not be construed as their endorsement of this book, Spilt Wine Publishing Company, or the website vintagewinepoems.com.

While the editorial opinions expressed in the introductions and "Back Label" sidebars are those of the editor, I did not come upon these brilliant insights, and their accompanying "facts", in a vacuum. The following were virtual treasure troves of information:

Wine, Women, and Song Medieval Latin Students' Songs; Now first translated into English Verse. John Addington Symonds, editor/translator. (London: Chatto and Windus, Piccadilly, 1884)

The Complete Poems Of Sir Thomas Moore Collected By Himself With Explanatory Notes, which includes: ***Odes Of Anacreon Translated Into English Verse With Notes*** (1800).

Poems From The Divan of Hafiz, translated by Gertrude Bell (1868-1926). (1897)

Rubaiyat of Omar Khayyam and Salaman and Absal Rendered Into English Verse By Edward FitzGerald – Centenary Edition (1909), contains some valuable comparison between direct translations of Khayyam and FitzGerald's renderings. This volume also contains an essay on Persian Poetry by Ralph Waldo Emerson.

The Works of Li Po, The Chinese Poet, Shigeyoshi Obata, translator/editor. (1921).

Fir-Flower Tablets: Poems Translated from the Chinese, translated. by Florence Ayscough (1878-1942), English versions by Amy Lowell (1874-1925) (1921).

Mytholgy, by Edith Hamilton (1867-1963), was originally published in 1942. This is still a great over-view of Greek, Roman, and Norse mythology. I first encountered it when I was in high school, and it has been a part of my library ever since. My most recent edition is from Back Bay Books, a division of Little, Brown and Company, the originagal publishers of the hard-bound edition of this classic. The copyright was renewed in 1969 by Dorian Fielding Reid and Doris Fielding Reid.

Bibliography:

American Poetry, 1922 A Miscellany, Edna St. Vincent Millay and Robert Frost, eds. (1922)
Fir-Flower Tablets: Poems Translated from the Chinese. translated. by Florence Ayscough, English versions by Amy Lowell (1921)
The Le Gallienne Book of English Verse, Richard Le Gallienne, editor (1922)
The Lyric Year: One Hundred Poems (1912)
The Oxford Book of English Verse, Chosen and Edited by Arthur Quiller-Couch (c. 1900)
The World's Best Poetry Vol. VIII: National Spirit, edited by Bliss Carman (1904)
The World's Best Poetry Volume IV, edited by Bliss Carman (1904)
Baudelaire: His Prose and Poetry, Thomas Robert Smith, editor (1919)
Poems by Elizabeth Barrett Browning (1844)
Sonnets from the Portuguese by Elizabeth Barrett Browning (1850)
An Ode to Harvard, and other poems by Witter Bynner (1907)
Grenstone poems: A sequence by Witter Bynner (1917)
Don Juan by Lord Byron (written 1819 -1824)
The Works of Lord Byron, Vol. 1, edited by Ernest Harley Coleridge, M.A. (1898)
Songs from Vagabondia by Bliss Carman and Richard Hovey (1894)
Song Spray by Thomas S. Collier (1889)
The Works of Abraham Cowley Vol I (1806)
At Dawn And Dusk, by Victor Daley (1898)
Wine and Roses, by Victor Daley and Bertram Stevens (1911)
Youth Riding by Mary Carolyn Davies (1919)
The Poems And Prose Of Ernest Dowson
The Poems of Ernest Dowson, edited by Arthur Symons and Aubrey Beardsley (1905)
The Complete Poems Of Paul Laurence Dunbar (1922)

Poems "Household Edition" by Ralph Waldo Emerson (1911)
Poems From The Divan of Hafiz, edited and translated by Gertrude Bell (1897)
Poems by William Henley (1920)
The Hesperides & Noble Numbers by Robert Herrick (1898)
The Poetical Works Of Oliver Wendell Holmes (1893)
John Keats: Poems Published in 1820 (1909)
Rubaiyat of Omar Khayyam, Rendered into English Verse by Edward FitzGerald – Fifth Edition (1889)
Amores: Poems by D. H. Lawrence (1916)
Robert Louis Stevenson And Elegy and Other Poems Mainly Personal by Richard Le Gallienne (1895)
Men, Women and Ghosts by Amy Lowell (1916)
Sword Blades and Poppy Seed by Amy Lowell (1914)
Wine, Women, and Song Mediaeval Latin Students' Songs; John Addington Symonds, editor/translator (1884)
Poetical Works by John Milton
The Complete Poems of Sir Thomas Moore (includes "Odes of Anacreon" - 1800)
The Works of Li Po The Chinese Poet; Shigeyoshi Obata, editor/translator (1921)
Lustra of Ezra Pound, including Cathay by Ezra Pound (1916)
The Poetical Works of Matthew Prior (1835)
Poems by Alan Seeger (1916)
A Child's Garden of Verses & Underwoods Ballads by Robert Louis Stevenson (1895)
New Poems by Robert Louis Stevenson (1918)
The Silverado Squatters by Robert Louis Stevenson (1883)
Rivers to the Sea by Sara Teasdale (1915)
The Poems of William Watson (1893)
Poems Of Passion by Ella Wheeler Wilcox (1883)
Responsibilities and Other Poems by William Butler Yeats (1917)
The Wild Swans At Coole by Williaim Butler Yeats (1919)

Picture Credits:
Front cover drawing by Edmund J. Sullivan, from *The Rubaiyat of Omar Khayyam: Illustrated Edition* (public domain)

"A picture of corks", which serves as the introduction to the section "Final Toasts" (p. 107) is licensed under the Creative Commons 3.0 License. (en.wikipedia.org/wiki/File:Corks019.jpg)

Illustration of a thyrsus, which accompanies "The Thyrsus: To Franz Liszt" by Charles Baudelaire (p. 84), was found in numerous locations on the web. None of these overtly revealed the drawing's origin.

vintagewinepoems.com

    Bottled Poetry: Verses *from the Vine,* is part of a larger project that includes the website, vintagewinepoems.com. This website was put together to provide the wine-drinking public, wine professionals, and wine writers with a source for poetry that celebrates wine. In the beginning, the one criteria for a wine poem being archived at this website was that it be in the pubic domain, that is, that it's copyright had expired and not been renewed – a criteria that I wished all poetry websites honored. Thus, the "vintage" wine poems in these pages were for the most part first published before 1923 and includes poets that are the most revered in the history of prosody.[*]

    This is not to say that wine poetry stopped at the dawn of the 20th Century – far from it! "Wine poems" have fermented from the pens (and later the typewriters and computer keyboards) of some of the most famous names in modern verse: Edna St. Vincent Millay, Pablo Neruda, Richard Wilbur, Dannie Abse, Billy Collins . . . add to these the many modern English translations of noted wine poets such as Baudelaire, Li Bai, and Hafiz – and there is enough material here for another edition (or two) of "Bottled Poetry: Verses from the Vine" – hmmmm. (Keep an eye on vintagewinepoems.com for any future developments.)

    An ever-growing and ever-changing section of vintagewinepoems.com exists to promote modern poetry. These web pages feature copyrighted material from modern day poets and exists to showcase and promote their work.

---

[*]vintagewinepoems.com and *Bottled Poetry: Verses from the Vine* adhere to the copyright laws of the United States of America.

A Word on Words

It is an amazing comment upon our times, that at the very moment when our capabilities to communicate with one another are at their highest, our abilities to do so are at their lowest. I fear the magic of words is being lost to an entire generation. We are inundated by a modern hieroglyphics that substitutes emoticons, abbreviations, and acronyms for real words and whole sentences. It is no wonder that poetry, that art form where words really matter, has a smaller readership than in any time in the history of the printing press.*

  Acquiring an appreciation for poetry is not easy. As with wine, the poetic palate matures over time. A preference for the simple, fruity, and flowery evolves into an appreciation for more complex and subtle flavors – drier, if you will, something beyond the sweet and sugary. If *Bottled Poetry: Verses from the Vine* has accomplished one of it's most important missions, you, dear reader, have a new or renewed appreciation for poetry.

  This mission accomplished, the easiest place for you to turn is the internet. With a click of the mouse, not only will you be able to find more poetry from the poets presented here, but also a vast sampling that includes many of our finest poets of today (including audio and video renditions - the former being a modern-day enhancement that I hope to see available with all poetry books, including this one, in the near future). However, I highly recommend a trip to the bookstore, either by a traditional or electronic highways. Let the Internet be your starting point, with such sites as you will find in the "Acknowledgments" section of this book (see p. 139) or at vintagewinepoems.com.

  Books in your home provide a service that no ISP can. Books offer the possibility for discovery and sharing that is only possible in the three dimensional world of your home library. Even the awesome portability and storage capacity of the electronic book does not replace the impact of rows of books lined up on a shelf. This is especially important if you have children. No greater gift can you give them than accessibility to those thoughts, those stories . . . those words that move you and your imagination.

---

*There are signs of the resurgence of poetry. The popularity of the "rap" music genre has made budding young poets out of many a tween and teen. The emergence of "spoken word" artists, most widely known through the cable network HBO and its popular "Def Poetry" show which enjoyed 6 seasons on the network (2002 through 2007), is another modern interpretation of the "poet and his lyre".

Spilt Wine Publishing Company

SPECIAL ACKNOWLEDGMENTS

I must give a toast to those traditional purveyors of information and resources to the public, those libraries still made of mortar and stone: **The Library of the University of Memphis, The Memphis /Shelby County Public Libraries,** and **The Desoto County Public Libraries** (Mississippi). A special thanks to those dedicated librarians whom I pestered.

A special bottle of bubbly I owe to family and friends who read, appreciated, and critiqued my work, both as editor and poet. Brian Bass (son, extraordinaire), Liz Edmundson, Felicia Wicker, Debra Mateer and all my "FB" friends deserve a wine party for putting up with my test samples and providing "tasting notes".

A special click of the goblet goes to my latest roommate and friend, Eric Reynolds. Thanks for being the best landlord and friend a writer could have. Your tolerance of my early morning risings is appreciated . . . ROLL TIDE!

I also give acknowledgment to Alfred L. Jones, who never read a word from these pages, but whose friendship shaped me as a writer and a lover of literature like no other. I still hear your voice, my dear friend!

As I owe my late friend Al for the words in my heart, so I owe my brother Bill for the music in my soul. I will always proudly wear the moniker "Bill Bass' Little Brother".

www.ingramcontent.com/pod-product-compliance
Lightning Source LLC
Chambersburg PA
CBHW081457040426
42446CB00016B/3275